Supergrass

Editor: **Mike Evans**
Assistant Editor: **Humaira Husain**
Production Controller: **Candida Lane**
Picture Research: **Maria Gibbs**
Art Editor: **Valerie Hawthorn**
Design: **Ian Loats, Design Revolution**

Special thanks to: Maria Jeffries; Simon and Ginny at Parlophone;
Simon Blackmore; Keith Wozencroft;
Lucy and Sophie of Mansize fanzine.

For permission to use record sleeve artwork, thanks to:
Luke and Barny at Moody Painters (01865 244244)
Ian at Designers Republic (01142 754982)

First published in 1996 by
Hamlyn, an imprint of
Reed Consumer Books Limited,
Michelin House, 81 Fulham Road,
London SW3 6RB
and Auckland, Melbourne, Singapore and Toronto

Copyright © 1996 Reed International Books Limited

A Catalogue record for this book is available from the British Library
ISBN 0 600 58977 3

Printed and bound in Great Britain by
Butler & Tanner Ltd, Frome and London

Picture Acknowledgements

All Action: /Chris Floyd 76, /Sue Moore 61, 75 top,
/Justin Thomas 74 right
Piers Allardyce: 16, 50, 51 right, 51 left
British Broadcasting Corporation / photographic library:
20 insert below
Matt Bright: 12
Famous: /Felipe 32, /Rob Howard 49 centre, 49 left, 49 right
Chris Floyd: 8 left, 19, 20 main pic, 38, 58, 69 top,
70 below, 70 top
Steve Gillett: 30
Steve Gullick: 6, 22, 26
Bryn Jones: 10
London Features International: /Joe Bangay 56
Mansize fanzine: 34, 37, 45 below, 68 top, 68 below
Mercury Music Prize: 72, 73
Donald Milne: 7, 11, 13 right, 13 left, 31, 33, 77
The Moody Painters / The Designers Republic: 78 below,
78 top, 79 top, 79 below
Pat Pope: 28 right, 28 left
Redferns: 18 below, 60, 27, 42, 43, 42 top, 59, 63, 29 left
Retna: /Adrian Callaghan 40, /Steve Double, 57,
64 centre, 65 left, 65 right, 66 top, 66 below,
/Robin Francois 3, 36, 47, /Ed Sirrs, 4, 39, 55
Rex Features: 69 below, 71, 74 left, /Brian Rasic 67
Zoe Shardlow: 8 centre, 8 right, 9
S.I.N: /Steve Double 64, /Martyn Goodacre 17,
29 right, 41, 45 top, 46, 48, 53, /Tony Mott 5,
/Paul Stanley 21, 23, 35, /Roy Tee 15,18 top
Stephen Sweet: 14, 24, 25, 44, 54 below
Ian T Tilton: 62, 80
Lili Wilde: 52, 75 below

Supergrass

EVERETT TRUE

HAMLYN

CONTENTS

INTRODUCTION
'Let's Talk About Sex'   5

'TEENAGE KICKS FOR A NEW GENERATION'
A Bluffer's Guide To The Jennifers   15

'CAUGHT BY THE BUZZ'
The Early History Of Supergrass In Three Parts   27

'MORE COCK THAN DOODLE-DO'
Supergrass Go Top 20   39

'LENNY KRAVITZ SITTING ON THE TOILET'
Supergrass Go Top 10   47

'YOU'RE KIDDING ME!'
Supergrass Hit Number One   53

'SMOKE A FAG, PUT IT OUT'
Supergrass Feel 'Alright'   63

SOFA, SO GOOD
Supergrass Take On The World   71

DISCOGRAPHY   77

★★★★☆★★★★★★★★★★

Introduction
'Let's Talk About Sex'

Supergrass appear on the *Melody Maker* front cover . . . they get drunk with the 'Maker . . . the band play *Top Of The Pops* . . . and fantasise about seeing the cast of *Grangehill* naked . . . the *Melody Maker* goes out on the road with Supergrass . . . and they get drunk together, again . . . plus: "What Is Pop?" – a brief discussion . . .

'WE'RE JUST PRETTY BRICKIES'

THE first time *Melody Maker* put Supergrass on its cover (February '95), the journalists involved (David Bennun and myself) plied them with champagne and soft drugs, encouraged them to talk salaciously about sexual conquests and sexual fantasies, had them photographed in mascara and cling-film (with lipstick marks on their cheeks), referred to them as 'pretty brickies' and '*The Bash Street Kids* sinking into juvenile delinquency', waxed lyrical about acid and washing dishes . . . did everything but dwell on the band's music, in fact.

Although the music was by no means secondary, it seemed like it was simply a natural extension of the band's ebullient, shameless personalities. An instant fix. Pure pop thrillsville. Glam rock for the Nineties. Madness, updated and given a fresh set of cheekbones. A pure distillation of all the racier parts of the last 40 years of pop music. *Effortless*. Melodies you could sing along to within 10 seconds of hearing them. Words you could memorise in the seconds between sleep and wakefulness. *Skill*.

We were bored with streams of self-important, heads-up-buttocks, musicians content to say variations on the 'We just make music for ourselves, if anybody else likes it then that's a bonus, man' line. It was a sheer pleasure to chat with three such unashamedly horny, youthful boys (even if one of them was in his early twenties). Their music we could listen to whenever we liked. We didn't want to talk about *that*.

(Like, pop – it's about glitter smudging on tear-streaked faces, walking naked through Hyde Park at five in the morning, the smack of a fist hitting soft flesh on the escalator above you, any number of stacked girls in close-fitting catsuits, the slicked-back hair of Errol Flynn, desperation and licentiousness in semen-stained bedsheets, a stolen

All wrapped up . . . and nowhere to go?

Gaz in America, September 1995

Danny at the Duchess of York, Leeds

Mickey at the Leeds 'Duchess', 1994

conversation at twilight . . . anything and everything except for music, in fact. Never trust a band who can explain their songs, put dull flesh to the bare bone of their muse. Never trust a band who claim not to think of the outside world, of the glorious pursuit of artificialness, of lust and fame and powdered boys. Never trust a band who think that worthiness will win in the end. Pop is about NOW and pop is about LUCK and pop is all about the cruel reality of BEAUTY, whichever form it takes. Pop is Supergrass is pop is Supergrass. Sorry, I digress.)

A sample exchange between the band and magazine ran thus . . .

Mickey: *'We're just pretty brickies.'*

Danny: *'I used to be a labourer. It was just a house job, doing fittings for an extension.'*

Gaz: *'And the odd burglary.'*

It's hard to imagine the slender Danny lifting anything heavier than his eyebrows. Haven't you all given up your day-jobs?

Gaz: *'Yeah, yeah, we have. About six weeks ago. Kitchens, cafes, factories. Danny was a dinner lady.'*

Did you not feel like some kind of bizarre fetish object? Did you feel emasculated?

Danny: *'It was all good, clean, healthy fun. I really liked the atmosphere. No, I didn't give extra portions to the girls I fancied.'*

Is it easier to pull, now that you're no longer working as a labourer or a dinner lady?

Danny: *'Not really. It doesn't happen like that.'*

Well, the exchange went something like that . . .

We'd already heard the stories of drummer Danny being mobbed by streams of panting girls when Supergrass supported Blur at Alexandra Palace, a few months previous. (This, despite the fact the band didn't even have a record available at the

time. Perhaps Justine Elastica's championing of their soon-come debut single 'Caught By The Fuzz', making it Single Of The Week on Radio 1FM, had something to do with it. We doubt it, though. Girls will always mob boys who like girls who like boys like Danny. Because boys like Danny have cheekbones that are *lush.*)

We'd been fed the reports of how Danny and singer Gaz's previous band – the extremely precocious and saucy Jennifers from Oxford – used to beg girls from onstage to give them their phone numbers. And how they would play their guitars with shaving razors. We'd already been begged by our more lustful girl friends to take them along with us to the interview, having caught a glimpse of Gaz's outrageous sideburns and bassist Mickey's chubby good looks on the vid to 'Mansize Rooster'.

At last, we thought, here was an indie band who were as sexy as the music they created. At fucking last. We were fed up to the back teeth with all the spotty girl-wary insecure indie kids clutching plastic bags and a copy of *Gardener's Monthly*, sick to death of neanderthal louts with Mancunian accents whose only claim to sexual fame was the bushiness of their eyebrows and the extent to which seemed to be able to rip off Mick Jagger's pout.

Thus we only had one thing on our collective, salacious mind when we went down to photographer Steve Gullick's Islington studio with Harrod's bags full of champagne to talk to the boys – get 'em drunk, get their clothes off and get 'em to talk about . . . sex!

We wanted their sex, and we wanted plenty of it.

'SHOOT UPWARDS! HAVE A LAUGH!'

ANOTHER sample interchange during the interview ran like this . . .

A female friend fantasises about being in bed with all three of you at once.

'Who's that?' Danny inquires eagerly. 'Do you have her phone number?'

Do you think you'd ever do something like that?

Gaz: 'What's the horsepower like?'

Mickey: 'It's probably better in her head than the harsh reality of actually going to bed with three sweaty musicians.'

Gaz: 'I'd rather we had three separate beds and each of us went to bed with a separate woman. In the same room. And laughed at Danny afterwards.'

Danny looks wounded. 'Why would you laugh at me?'

'Dunno,' replies Gaz, 'you'd just be really funny. We'd probably pick up some tips on sexual technique from each other. I think Mickey'd be best.'

'Apparently,' reveals Danny, 'he's got big balls.'

'Have I?' Mickey sounds pleasantly surprised.

You mean you don't know?

'I might have five years' more experience,' Mickey allows, 'but most of that was spent wanking.'

So you've got your wanking technique down then? Both hands, as Shampoo might have it?

'It's something you get with age.'

What's your favourite sexual technique?

'Orgasm,' decides Mickey. 'I do like that.'

'Technique?' puts in an enthusiastic Gaz. 'Shoot upwards. Have a bit of a laugh. Funny things happen to everyone during sex. Like falling asleep because you're young and tired.'

Mickey, it emerges, lost his virginity at the national average (17), Gaz when he was 14 (he also thinks '69' is 'quite a nice position'). Danny can't even remember that far back.

'The first girl I ever snogged was probably Natalie Smith,' he recalls. 'It was behind her house, when I was about eight.

Bathtime – just good clean fun

Gaz (left) at the Princess Charlotte, Leicester, and Gaz, Danny and Mickey as they are known and loved

Her brother was involved, in the way it works at school. It was a sex training camp. The whole fucking primary school was at it. You'd practice on your mates' elder sisters... look, can we talk about something else, like the music?'

Oh, for fuck's sake. Alright.

NB: The band wouldn't have minded the resultant article's salaciousness, but they were concerned their mothers might read it. (*''Ere cum my mum/Well she no wot I've dun.'*) Which they did.

Danny, Gaz and Mickey barely escaped with their lives.

And thus another rock/pop legend was born.

'UNBELIEVABLY STUPID'

THE second time *Melody Maker* put Supergrass on its cover (May '95), the journalist Taylor Parkes called them the *'most unbelievably stupid band in the world'*. He intended this as a compliment,

incidentally. He then went on to call the group 'wankers' because Gaz wasn't sure whether appearing on the front cover of *Smash Hits* was such a good idea.

Gaz was more concerned that Supergrass songs should be seen to stand the test of time, that kids shouldn't just be into them because they fancied one of 'em. Taylor argued back that buying a record cos you fancy the guitarist and buying a record cos you like the guitar line are pretty much one and the same thing.

Pop music, to Taylor, must always, always be stupid – stupid, as in not understanding the rules, as in running blind, as in *stupid with desire*, stupid with joy, as in stupefied. Yeah, that kind of stupid.

What this was conveniently overlooking was that Gaz probably knows more about his rock heritage than most rock journalists combined – having spent the time in between his unsuccessful stint with The

Jennifers and the formation of Theodore Supergrass (as Supergrass were originally known) practicing his guitar licks to old Beatles, Jimi Hendrix, JJ Cale and Frank Zappa records. He might have initially been inspired to form a band by the success of fellow hometown shoegazers, the youthful Ride – but he quickly moved on to the source(s) of the music.

Mickey, too, is renowned for being a bit of a bedroom four-track tape specialist, having recorded literally hundreds of the fuckers, for want of anything better to do.

Danny – the lad who's been called 'a Keith Moon in the making' (after Sixties beat combo The Who's legendary and dead, hell-raising drummer) more often than most of us have had hot shags – is probably the one who correlates best to Taylor's summation of the band as 'stupid, like the heavens'.

But the other two? Mini-musos in the making. And, fuck it, why not, if it produces

'Here they come . . . The Jennifers!'

music this stunning, this seamless?

Anyway, here are two sample interchanges between the band and Taylor (the interview took place at the *Top Of The Pops* studios, during Supergrass' debut appearance on the show, for 'Lenny') . . .

Some members of the **Grange Hill** *cast walk past and start giggling at us.*

Danny's eyes almost tumble into his lap.

'Look! The cast of **Grange Hill**! *Let's see if we can get them naked.'*

And the second . . .

Gaz: *'. . . I just remember my birthday party, with my cake in front of me and Wham! playing somewhere in the background.'*

Mickey: *'You had Wham! at your birthday party? Wow!'*

Danny: *'I loved all that stuff, though! Kajagoogoo! I used to lure girls back to my bedroom and play them Kajagoogoo, trying to get a snog.'*

Did they ever go for it?

'Nah.'

Why not?

'They were too shy.'

For over 10 minutes, Danny can't work out why everyone else around the table has just laughed themselves purple. Finally, realisation spreads across his face like dawn breaking.

NB: The band wouldn't have minded being typecast again, except they couldn't understand why they needed to appear on the front of *The Maker* twice.

'But we've already done that one,' they wailed to their press agent, while he patiently tried to explain how press campaigns worked.

Taylor probably would've been well reassured in his quest for stupidity in Supergrass' music if he'd heard the rumour about where the title for 'Lenny' came from. The song was (supposedly) originally called 'Around And Around' – after its chorus – until a friend remarked that the song sounded like 'Lenny Kravitz sitting on the toilet'. Hence the change of title.

Incidentally, the band are all big fans of Lenny Kravitz's second album . . . now that really *is* stupid.

Mr Gareth Coombes | **Mr Daniel Goffey**

'BIT OF AN EVERYTHING MAN'

THE first time I went on the road with Supergrass (March '95), Danny and I ended up getting into a fist fight at an after-show party in Brighton. What was it about? Can't remember. Some girl or other, probably. Who won? Can't remember. Although I do recall several large tables of drinks ending up sprawled on the floor.

Were we still mates afterwards? Of course.

Alcohol and hedonism goes to everyone's heads once in a while, and it's best to sort it out while you're still throbbing and the thrill is hot. Or something.

Here's how I described Danny at the time…

Thu, 00.50, Lorne Park Hotel (Glasgow)
. . . a bottle of Jack is produced, and the band look on bemused as it gets quaffed in 10 minutes flat by – ooh – at least four of us.

''Ere,' asks a bewildered Danny, finally, 'I thought it was us who were meant to behave like that.'

Danny, of course, is the one member of Supergrass who does almost live up to their popular image of being hedonistic, babe-lovin', cocaine-sniffin' wide boys. The other two have girlfriends – and anyway, Mickey's far too old for such nonsense. Danny's the one you can rely on

to invite everyone back up to his shared hotel room, the one who'll get off with members of Shampoo, the one who'll gently chide the Maker for its flamboyant approach to interviewing and then ask in his devilishly soft voice which drugs we prefer. (And then tell us he's a 'bit of an everything man himself'!) Danny, as we have already indicated, is a Keith Moon in the making – without any of the boorish elements. Every group needs a member like Danny.

Shame then that it should be Danny who gets the fan letters from wannabe drummers, while it's Gaz who finds

himself surrounded by nubile, thrusting young 'Gazettes' – see Edinburgh.

The last we remember is ordering a quadruple Peach Schnapps, no ice, until…

Thu, 19.30, Edinburgh University bar

Danny is sitting at the T-shirt stall, licking each poster bought. Yeah, that's right – licking them. 'How much for a signed one,' a female admirer asks salesman Mike Swag. 'A quid extra,' he replies, quick as a flash, before picking up his pen with a theatrical flourish and writing 'With love from Mick Swag'.

'That's gonna be worth a fortune in a couple of years,' Danny informs her, tongue at the ready.

The fan pays up, and departs bemused.

NB: The band didn't mind being written about this way at all this time. Because, by now, I'd gotten round to describing their music as well, describing them as the new Madness, in terms of chart longevity, new Slade in terms of terrace friendliness, new Buzzcocks in terms of a relentless riff, new Nirvana if only cos Mickey's basslines are so sizeable, new Who cos drummer Danny is the Nineties Keith Moon or I'm a brainless Sleeper acolyte, new Blur cos I've been told to write that, new Monkees in terms of teen appeal, new Mungo Jerry for the sideburns…

Yes, you could say I was more than impressed by their live show. Twenty minutes of non-stop hits, including one absolute stormer of a song – yet to be released at that point – called 'Alright', which featured the most insidiously catchy two-note piano solo any side of a Chas'N'Dave medley. Plus 'Caught By The Fuzz', 'Mansize Rooster' (which is Madness snorting crystal meth on the back of a school bus, or I'm a stuffed, pickled turkey), the *illin'* 'Lenny'… and all the other numbers which would go to make up *the* Debut Album Of 1995, No Argument Sonny Or I'll Chin Ya, the frankly *fresh* 'I Should Coco'.

YOUR ASS IS 'GRASS!

BUT, hold up! I'm getting carried away, over-excited, ahead of myself. There's a severe danger of premature ejaculation looming from underneath the satin and saliva.

You want to know where Supergrass come from, who they snogged at kindergarten, whether The Jennifers really were as bad as everyone says now, how Gaz found the audacity to grow those Monkey Man sideburns, whether it's really true that Danny's dad occasionally presents BBC2's *Top Gear*, who the mysterious Mike Swag is, how the 'Grass came to be on the same record label as Cliff Richard and The Pet Shop Boys, which member it was who had matching foot tattoos done with the singer of Powder, which one's got a kid, who got asked by Calvin Klein to model their underwear, and just what . . .

Basically, you want to turn to the second chapter.

And you want to turn there NOW!

'Teenage Kicks For A New Generation'
A Bluffer's Guide To The Jennifers

The formative secrets of Supergrass are revealed : . . . Danny was a dinner lady . . . Gaz started growing his sideburns at 14 . . . Mickey was a bedroom tape 'saddo' . . . Wheatley Park Comprehensive : the definitive history . . . and were the Jennifers really as bad as everyone says? . . . plus loads and loads more stuff about pop . .

WHO WERE THE JENNIFERS?

AT the time of their *Melody Maker* interview in August 1992, they were Gareth Coombes (vocals, 16); Andy Davies (bass, 17); and brothers Nick and Danny Goffey (guitar, 20, and drums, 18, respectively). All lived in Oxford. The Jennifers released one single, 'Just Got Back Today', on Suede's label Nude, and split up in the face of overwhelming critical indifference a few months afterwards.

Gareth ('Gaz') and Danny later went on to form Supergrass.

WERE THEY AS BAD AS EVERYONE MAKES OUT?

I GUESS so. Someone played a couple of their songs to me down the phone the other day – the first time I'd ever heard The Jennifers – and they sounded like all the worst aspects of the Thames Valley shoegazing scene and late Sixties wah-wah guitar solo overkill rolled into one. With the additional bonus of a song The Bluetones would've killed at birth.

Mind you, the line was quite crackly.

AND . . .?

ONE *Melody Maker* critic quoted French post-modernist Jean Beaudrillard at them, before going on to say this about their Camden Falcon show, in July 1992: 'I wouldn't call them a rock band because that might imply an understanding of tradition and continuity, of finding new ways to express a common source. Instead I'll call them a "beat combo" . . . the most complacent and depressing gig since Dodgy . . . if anyone tells you they're "happening", don't believe another word they write, ever. I mean that.'

Ex-*MM* Assistant Editor Steve Sutherland, meanwhile, wrote this about the band he saw supporting Thousand Yard Stare at The

The Jennifers (left) live on stage, and Supergrass live backstage

Gaz holds a ball

Ride at the Royal Albert Hall

Venue, New Cross, in April '92: 'It's hard to say what The Jennifers are like just now. They're so new, so young, so wet behind the ears, so timidly emerging from their Ride obsession, that any solid judgement would surely be premature.'

HEDGING HIS BETS, THEN
YES.

WHAT DID THEIR PR SAY ABOUT THEM?
'YOU'D be forgiven for thinking their influences were post-Valentines, but you'd be wrong: The Jennifers' sound owes more to The Searchers and Neil Young, to Pink Floyd and The Who and to psychedelic pop in general than it does to Ride, Blur and a dozen other soundalikes . . .

'The title song is surely teenage kicks for a new generation. And with it, The Jennifers suggest a maturity way beyond their years.'

(*Best In Press* press release for 'Just Got Back Today')

AND NOW . . ?
'THE single was quite accomplished considering they were about 15. I'm sure I wasn't capable of anything like that at the age of 15.'

(Simon Blackmore, Parlophone PR)

SO WHAT WAS THE SINGLE REALLY LIKE?
(*MM* July '92, Singles Reviews): ' . . . like most 14-year-olds, The Jennifers are

incorrigible chancers. Most of this sounds like Blur on a very bad day. The title track is a quiet mournful love song that is vaguely reminiscent of The La's and The Stone Roses . . . overall, though, it's a bit cold and empty, like they know only too well what's expected.'

SO THEY DIDN'T GET MUCH GOOD PRESS
THAT'S not quite fair.

Check this report of their Leeds gig from the pages of *Melody Maker*, August '92: ' A very good pop group who could easily become a great one . . . although their influences figure prominently on their sleeves (Byrds, Hendrix, Roses, Charlatans), they have a corking big guitar sound and no small amount of tunes. They also have a striving, yearning quality that smacks of musical (as opposed to personal, ego-led) ambition . . . but do change that name, lads.'

(An unusually prescient Dave Simpson)

HOW DID THEY RESPOND TO CRITICISM?
GARETH: 'What does it matter how old we are? All we do is play music and enjoy it. If anything, it's a much bigger advantage to be young. We've got so much time to write

songs. We're not fakes. We have never written a song to sound like anybody. Soon people will understand our vibe.'

(*MM* 'Advance' feature, August 1992)

POP POTENTIAL?

OH, definitely.

'A potential male bombshell in the Tim Burgess and Mark Gardener line,' according to Oxford boy, *The Maker's* Ben Turner.

Tim is the singer with Hammond-drenched Northerners The Charlatans. He pouts too much for his own good. Mark is the singer with dreamy, guitar-laden OX2 rockers Ride.

He pouts too much for his own good, too.

Gaz doesn't need to. He is – how you put it? – telegenic.

Extremely.

WHAT WAS YOUR DEFINITION OF POP AGAIN?

I'M glad you asked.

Nancy Sinatra's boots; the noise a cat makes when it's sleeping; cheekbones and sideburns and tightly creased polyurethane trousers; Chris Evans turned down low, with the sun just filtering in; Astro Boy stickers; Astro Girl stickers; Speed Racer stickers; Mariah Carey with the sound off and on constant pause; buttons ripped off in anger; a video camera out-of-focus on the Empire State Building; Audrey Hepburn's cigarette holder; Plastic Fantastic's PVC-clad arses; the noise a cat makes when it's waking; scratchy old 45s left in their sleeves; Mike Swag, Supergrass' salesman *extraordinaire*.

Pop should never be seen to be forced, it should always *aspire*. Pop should always be creating that *little bit of something* that wasn't there before, that something which makes life that little bit tangier, sharper, glitzier. Pop is Marc Almond's diamond flashes and Michelle Gayle's skirt, the girl in the Paul Weller video, running helplessly through the meadows. (Pop is NOT NOT NOT Paul Weller though, all grunty exhortations and workmanlike sweat. Pop would rather be seen shagging the corpse of funk-metal than have anything to do with Paul Weller. Pop is plastic – not wooden.)

Pop is pop is pop. Pop is about context and time and placing . . . and Supergrass, more than anyone during 1995, WERE pop. Except TLC, maybe.

And if you can remember them, you most definitely weren't there.

Alright?

On set at the Italian-style Welsh village of Port Merion, for the 'Alright' video

Mirror-gazing on the 'Alright' shoot, and (inset) Danny's dad Chris Goffey

ALRIGHT. SO HOW ABOUT SOME HISTORY?

FAIR enough, squire.

Let's deal with Gaz first.

Like the other members of Supergrass, Gaz is actually from what could only be called a staunchly middle-class background. His mother is an English teacher and his father is a food scientist who runs his own diagnostics firm 'who look at chemicals in food and loads of complicated things like that'. Right from an early age, he was surrounded by music and musical instruments – in fact his dad is rumoured to play a mean line in boogie-woogie piano. (His elder brother Bobsie plays piano with Supergrass on tour.)

Gaz was presented with his very first guitar when he was just 11 years old, and made his debut demos a year later with the help of a friend who played piano. By the time he was 13, he'd got shot of that particular friend and brought in a bass player, plus Danny on drums. Danny, who was a couple of years above Gaz at Wheatley Park Comprehensive, was introduced to the singer via Bobsie, who was in the same year at school as the drummer. At first, Danny didn't really want anything to do with his future frontman.

'I thought he was a little dick, actually,' he admitted to the *NME*. 'No, in fact, I didn't even have an opinion on him, really. He was just some kid a couple of years below us. I knew his brother, but Gaz... I don't know. Who was he?'

Within six months the trio were gigging around the Oxford area, playing things like covers of Smiths and Cure songs, a wild version of the American post-hardcore band Dinosaur Jr's 'Freak Scene', and even one of their own compositions, 'You Keep Punching Me'. (Gaz claims this is still one of his personal favourites.)

Andthe band's name? They decided to call themselves The Jennifers.

Not even old enough to be able to drink legally, they were soon to know the fickle attentiveness of fame and the resultant years of wilderness.

VERY ATMOSPHERIC. SO WHAT ABOUT DANNY?

I WAS just coming to that.

Danny's past is a little more mysterious.

His father, Chris Goffey, is a motoring correspondent who occasionally presents BBC2's *Top Gear* car show. And, according to *The Maker* cover story done to celebrate Supergrass' inclusion on Sub Pop's Shelter housing charity benefit EP, 'Helter Shelter', his mother was a Labour councillor who took

him to see a few dates on the Red Wedge (a coalition of left wing rock musicians in the early Eighties) tour when he was still at junior school.

'I remember seeing one show and it was Paul Weller, Billy Bragg, Rik Mayall and Tracey Ullman,' he told *The Maker's* Ian Gittins. 'It was alright, actually.

'I moved to Oxford when I was 14,' Danny told *Select* magazine in Jun '95, 'and my brother asked me if I'd play drums with this

'The next round's on you . . .'

Live at the Oxford Apollo, February 1995

'At 10,' he told *Q* magazine, 'I was signing autographs in return for a peek at girls' knickers. I know the score.'

SO WHAT'S OXFORD LIKE TO GROW UP IN?

ACCORDING to journalist Ben Turner, it's 'a town that doesn't change, no matter how long you leave it'. Lots of scarf-clad students. Dreaming spires. Quaint English architecture. Tea shops. Punting on the river. Wildean. *Cultured.* Not exactly conducive to rock'n'roll – even if you do take the joy-riding council estate dwellers into consideration.

Healthy rave scene, though.

Apparently.

DID THE JENNIFERS TOUR THE UK?

YES. The Jennifers' debut UK tour began in June '92.

By that point they'd already played 50 shows.

SO HOW DID THEY MANAGE TO ATTEND SCHOOL AND GIG AT THE SAME TIME?

GOOD question.

They didn't. Not really.

'The Jennifers fucked my education, you know,' Danny informed *NME* in April '95. 'In the end it got embarrassing because I was never there and school just sort of suggested that I leave.'

There again, it might not have been just The Jennifers' fault.

He told *Melody Maker's* Ian Gittins that when he was 15 he got expelled for being . . . *naughty.* But I never told my mum. I'd go out each morning like I was going to school, but then, instead, I'd go to this travellers' site that was on the way to school and hang out with the kids there all day.

'I spent about three weeks doing that,' he added, 'but then I got found out when my mum phoned up the school. She asked them when the Parent's Evening was, and they said, "Why should you want to know? We kicked your son out three weeks ago!"'

'It was good times,' remembered Gaz fondly in i-D. 'There'd be the reality check of coming back home from a gig and looking at

---

bloke in the first year. That was Gaz. I don't know if we *liked* each other…'

'Of course we did,' interrupted Gaz, hurt.

' . . . it was fate,' he continued. 'We've got good karma together.'

By the time that Gaz was going on 15, The Jennifers had signed with the indie Nude label and their line-up now included Danny's brother Nick on guitar and a close friend called Andy on bass.

ANY PREVIOUS CONVICTIONS?

DANNY was asked by a *Melody Maker* writer whether he thought that all pop groups should start off during their late teens.

'That should be the END of their careers!' he retorted, snobbily. 'I started off when I was 10 – The Fallopian Tubes, man, great band, "My Wife Shut My Gonads In The Door". That one was about sexual frustration, I seem to recall. So were all the others…

your homework at one in the morning. Because we were so young, we got treated as a novelty in the press, and they'd go on about "Gaz and his stick-on sideburns". Mind you, they still do.'

Indeed. *Unique* asked Gaz in June '95 what he had to say in their defence.

'Oh gawd!' he moaned. 'I've said this in every single interview I've ever done, man. I've had them since I was 14. On a smaller

band's debut single, 'Just Got Back Today' b/w 'Rocks And Boulders', 'Danny's Song' and 'Tomorrow's Rain', produced by Chris Hufford, (who has also worked with Radiohead, Slowdive, Chapterhouse and others), appeared in August 1992. It didn't exactly so much flop as sink without trace.

'We'd just signed Suede and everything went immediately mad,' Galpern told Record Collector in July '95. 'I suppose The

SO WHAT WENT WRONG?

A CLASSIC example of too much, too young.

It's all very well forming your first rock band and playing live shows when you're only 14, but your muse has to draw on *something*. The Jennifers were clearly too much in thrall to local heroes Ride and other dreadfully dated shoegazing bands like The Charlatans and Blur (who were going through a helluva lean patch at the time) to

More backstage relaxation in luxurious dressing rooms

scale, of course. It was never a fashion statement. I was just pleased that I could grow them. Not many people could. I just kept them.'

CAN WE HAVE A WORD FROM THEIR EX-LABEL BOSS?

SURE. Inspired by the example of Ride, The Jennifers signed a two-single deal with Saul Galpern, owner of London indie, Nude, somewhere around the start of 1992. The

Jennifers took second place, though I thought they were really good. Then I remixed their single before it was released, and they didn't like it. It was the summer that Gaz left school, and he didn't really know what to do. So I suggested that they go off and find a direction. Which is what they've done.'

WAS THERE A SECOND SINGLE?

NO. The Jennifers split up somewhere around the beginning of 1993.

ever amount to anything any good.

A neat line in duplicating Hendrix solos doesn't compensate, either.

WHAT'S THE BAND'S EXCUSE FOR ALL THIS?

DANNY: 'We were just little fishes. The Jennifers were a school band, a YTS band. Dealing with executive people when you're 15, 16 sits in your mind a bit. We needed to grow up. The two or three years that have gone in-between are the two years when you learn a lot in life.'

'Formative years,' agrees Gaz, 'of shit jobs and drugs and male bonding. There were no great tragedies, no great angst. We just grew up as people and as musicians.'

OK, I GET THE PICTURE. THE JENNIFERS REALLY WEREN'T VERY GOOD, WERE THEY? SO WHERE DOES MICKEY FIT INTO ALL THIS?

AFTER The Jennifers disbanded, not much happened for several months. Gaz and Danny retreated to their respective homes in Oxford, fingers burnt, vowing not to re-emerge until they were truly ready.

Gaz spent his days practising in his bedroom to Hendrix, Beach Boys and Beatles records and developing those mutton chop sideburns. Danny – a rock'n'roller even back then – avoided rehearsing as much as possible, and got a string of jobs, including his infamous stint as a dinner lady at a sixth form girls school.

'I used to serve mashed potato and stuff,' he told *Time Out* in February '95. 'The mashed potato scoop gave me a sore thumb at first, but then I built up thumb muscles.'

'I used to wash up in a hotel, and, before that, in a beer-bottle factory,' Gaz added. 'Still, you need a bit of misery to make you go out and write great songs.'

The pair began rehearsing in a Wheatley cottage with Tara Milton, former singer with neo-Mod classicists 5:30 (Gaz: 'We always said that if The Jennifers ever fucked up, we'd still work together. It was quite romantic. We had candlelight and everything'). It was around this time that the singer got a job at the local Harvester restaurant, where he met guitarist Mickey Quinn, five years his elder.

THE MIGHTY QUINN, HUH?

YEAH. The mighty Quinn.

At 22, Mickey didn't have the foggiest idea what he wanted to do, where his life was going. He'd spent two years on a computer course at Brighton Polytechnic before dropping out. He'd travelled abroad –

Danny puts his feet up

including a six-month stint backpacking through North Australia in a beaten-up old truck when he was 18. By day, he did whatever odd job presented itself ('shit caff jobs, that sort of thing'). By night, he'd record tapes and tapes of weird shit on a borrowed four-track in his bedroom at his parent's house in Wheatley. He kept his artistic muse alive by playing bass and guitar with local psychedelic reggae, folk and whoever's-available groups.

His dad, a scientist who does 'weird research shit with cells and stuff', and his ex-

social worker mother, used to wonder what he did alone in his room for such long periods of time. So did he.

Then one day, the younger brother of his old schoolfriend Bobsie Coombes, began work at the same restaurant as him. Mickey already knew who Gaz was, having seen – and enjoyed – The Jennifers on a number of occasions.

'I remember watching them at Forest Hill Hall,' he told *Q* in October '95. 'The only lighting they had was two strobes, which were on throughout the whole show. They played stuff like Dinosaur Jr covers, and Danny was doing all these crap drum rolls.'

Whatever. When Mickey was asked by the youthful guitarist whether he'd like to go down and jam with him, plus ex-Jennifers drummer Danny and singer Tara, he replied in the affirmative. It wasn't as if he had anything much else to do.

So he went down to a rehearsal and jammed a few times as the other guitarist, with Tara on bass. It was good – great, in fact, far above what any of them had managed up until then – but something wasn't right. There were too many egos, too many frontmen. Too many clashing personalities, which distracted from the music. So Mickey, Danny and Gaz decided to get together and have a few rehearsals without Tara. They clicked, big time. And thus (Theodore) Supergrass were born.

And how did Tara feel about this? Fine. He was already jamming with other musicians, the nucleus of which went on to form The Nubiles. And he's extremely happy that his former partners are doing so well.

Apparently.

THAT'S LUCKY

YEAH. You and me might feel the odd smidgeon of jealousy, but what the heck. The Nubiles are a damn good band in their own right – a dark emotional outpouring which manifests itself through sweet, sweet harmonies and an instinctive understanding of the great power of repetition. Tara wears the coolest beret this side of Jane Russell, and his band's live shows are often inspirational. You should check their records out… like NOW!

Anyway, back to the main story.

If Gaz is the main inspiration behind Supergrass – the precocious, talented member – and Danny is the wild card, then Mickey is definitely the group's calming influence, the one who keeps their feet somewhere near the ground. He also claims to be the only one not to smoke dope (he smoked it for too many years and it made him paranoid).

'I don't think I've got any influence on

Gaz gives it to 'em

them at all,' he told the *NME*. 'Gaz is the most mature 19-year-old in the world anyway, and Danny – I freak Danny out sometimes and tell him he's a cunt, but he's not the subtlest of geezers.'

That's for sure.

ANY WORD FROM THE PRESS?

'THE Jennifers may have stood alone with the dreams of children, but the dreams soured too soon in a flurry of accusation of lack of commitment and dragging dead wood… for every interminable two-chord wah-wah chunder, there was a 'Just Got Back Today' or that great, throbbing, nameless object that was apparently going to be the second single. And then – a big fat nothing. Until now. Those Goffey siblings are back with a new bassman as Theodore Supergrass. So, yes, they're a trio, vaguely late Sixties-ish threads and all, and a huge quantity of facial hair on the singer. They've been hanging out with Tara, ex-5:30 man and now head Nubile, and boy-oh-boy it shows.'

(From Oxford's *Curfew* magazine, November '93)

WHAT ARE THE OTHER JENNIFERS DOING NOW?

NICK Goffey directs the Supergrass videos. He's the bloke responsible for getting Gaz into a dress for the 'Mansize Rooster' vid, the one who came up with the bright primary Seventies appeal of 'Alright', the one who managed to convince the band to take a bath naked in blue goo for 'Mansize Rooster'.

He's also been filming Supergrass for the past year on Super-8, for use in a future film.

Andy Davies, meanwhile, is a student at Bristol University.

SO, FINALLY. IS GAZ REALLY REPENTANT ABOUT HIS PAST?

ARE you kidding?

'I listen to The Jennifers' single sometimes,' Gaz told *The Observer* magazine in August 1995. 'I really think it's quite good.'

★★★★★★★★★★★★★★★★★

'Caught By The Buzz'
The Early History Of Supergrass In Three Parts

The early secrets of Supergrass revealed: . . . the producer, the press agent and the A&R man . . they support Blur, Ride and get compared to The Cardiacs . . . the story behind 'Caught By The Fuzz' . . . the converted millhouse in Cornwall . . . and more pop!

PART ONE: SAM WILLIAMS (SUPERGRASS PRODUCER)

AROUND the time Theodore Supergrass started rehearsing, a musician-producer called Sam Williams bumped into the fledgling band in a local music store.

Sam had recently moved up to Oxford from Cornwall, where he'd been helping engineer and produce stuff for both his own and other bands at the Sawmills studio, a converted millhouse located on the mouth of a wooded creek.

Supergrass producer Sam Williams

Sam's band The Mystics

'I first saw them in a music shop,' he told *Melody Maker's* Tom Doyle in June '95, 'and I was suddenly surrounded by this gang of children with strange facial hair and strange clothes – they were wearing massive sorts of flared velvet trousers and stuff and they had these faces that you've only seen on Sixties albums. They were a dense little vibe, kind of giggling, and making a lot of a racket.'

Sam struck up a rapport with the band after promising to play them some recordings he'd made with his own group (The Mystics, who are now signed to Fontana: Sam's their singer).

'A while later,' he continued, 'I went to see them playing in this tiny little pub. Suddenly, there was the three of them crammed into a corner with their gear and they whacked into "Strange Ones" and there was just this serious energy. Even though it was hard to hear the songs clearly, you could tell there was an intelligence there, loads of interesting little tempo changes and stuff.'

Excited by what he'd witnessed, Sam offered to go round to Gaz's house and record some demos with the band. So, in November 1993, he went up to the cottages where they all lived in Wheatley.

'It was weird', he told Tom Doyle, 'because it was a bit like that scene out of *Help!* where The Beatles walk into four separate doors that all lead into one house – they all had cottages next to each other.'

Sam would set up his four-track tape recorder in the middle of Danny's tiny bedroom while the band would get a fire going, smoke some reefer, open a few bottles of red wine, and race through a couple of songs at full speed. (Half the songs which appeared on Supergrass' debut album 'I Should Coco' were demo-ed in the two final months of 1993.)

'What did Sam Williams teach us?' Danny was asked by one magazine. 'He taught us how to frame a song a bit better, and he taught us how to laugh and smoke joints. Or did we teach him?'

Upon hearing the tapes, Sawmills offered the band a production deal, and, on February 9th 1994, the band and Sam Williams went down to Cornwall to begin recording some 'proper' demos.

Sawmills is a suitably strange place for Supergrass to record in: it's an old millhouse by the side of an disused railway line, converted into accommodation for bands, with the studio downstairs and the bedrooms and living quarters upstairs, where everyone hangs out and plays pool. Situated off the estuary of The Fowey river, the only way to get to it is either by boat or by foot. It's a great place to escape to and chill out for a while.

Anyway, the band managed to record everything quite fast during this first session – just picking on the songs which had come out best during the original demos in Danny's bedroom – and within a week, they had six songs demo-ed: 'Caught By The Fuzz', 'Strange Ones', 'Mansize Rooster', 'Sitting Up Straight', 'Lose It' and 'Alright' (a couple of which would be pressed into future use as B-sides).

Sam took a tape of these demos to Oxford's Courtyard Management, (home of Parlophone signings, local boys Radiohead) who gave it to Keith Wozencroft, A&R rep for Parlophone in London.

And so it was, in June 1994, that Supergrass came to be signed to a major label.

INTERRUPTION ONE
WHAT is pop?

'I'd have a sex change if I could go and shag myself afterwards,' says Gaz, taking a hefty swig of champagne.

'If Gaz had a sex change, he'd be all right,' Mickey concurs. 'He wore a blonde wig and a beauty spot in the video [to

Radiohead vocalist Thom

Keep those campfires burning

Live on stage at Glastonbury

"Mansize Rooster'" He was gorgeous. Couldn't believe it. Bit toothy – but in a Joanna Lumley way.'

'They were gasping for it,' counters the singer, spliffing up. 'They kept touching up my arse in the make-up room.'

'I wouldn't kick Danny out of bed if he had a sex change,' comments Mickey, 'but I'm not asking him to.'

He pauses for unsober reflection.

'He'd probably kick me out of bed, though.'

Danny: 'If I was a girl, I'd fancy Mickey.'

Why?

'He'd give me the stability I need.'

(From the pages of *Melody Maker*, February 11th, 1995)

PART TWO: KEITH WOZENCROFT (PARLOPHONE A&R)

IN April 1994, Parlophone's A&R rep Keith Wozencroft went down to watch Supergrass rehearse in Wheatley Park, encouraged by Chris Hufford and Bryce Edge of Courtyard Management.

'What attracted me to them was their energy and songs,' Keith told me recently. 'I went down to this little shed near Oxford, a garage type place where they used to practise, and they played six songs . . .

'What was amazing,' he continued, 'was that not only did they have an energy and humour which made them stand out, but also that the songs were great, with the backing vocals and harmonies all in place. And when they stopped playing and we started chatting, they were very sussed people, their musical references were very wide.

'I'd seen The Jennifers a few times in London, but there wasn't anything particularly special about them,' he recalled. 'The Jennifers, musically, lay somewhere between that M4 shoegazing scene and Suede, I guess. Having said that, however, my attitude towards A&R is that if you come across a bunch of 15-years-olds with the potential of The Jennifers you should keep an eye on them.

Telephone   Phonecard

Waiting for the call

An early band pic with some lovely knitwear

'My first impressions of Supergrass as individuals is as they are now. Danny is a real laugh, quite unpredictable. Mickey's the elder one, one of the easier guys to talk to, always listening to what you're saying, making decisions in his head, very questioning. And Gaz is just a real casual guy, the sort of guy you just want to have a beer with in the pub.

'When I first talked with them about music, they mentioned stuff from The Stones to The Sex Pistols, The Jam to Steve Harley's Cockney Rebel, Van Morrison to weirder stuff like Gong, anyone who's put out great records, they'd sucked it all in. I'm 32 and a lover of music, and to be able to talk about it on the same level as 18, 19-year-olds is really quite impressive.

'What I liked about them wasn't so much their sex appeal as their energy, which will always appeal to young audiences. I thought they'd have a young fanbase thing going with the kids in college, but that they'd also be a rock band who would cross over to a wider audience, cos they were great songwriters.'

INTERRUPTION TWO
WHAT is pop?

Supergrass, Shampoo and Cliff Richard – spot the connection?

All are signed to EMI Records, which august institution held its annual conference in Brighton late last year. Supergrass' first single, 'Caught By The Fuzz', was just out – an autobiographical tale of Bash Street Kids *sinking into juvenile delinquency. Key-line, so to speak: '*Here comes my mum/She knows what I've done.*' Oh, the shame.*

'It was just a real fucked night, man,' understates Gaz. 'We went along and there were all these famous faces – Robert Palmer over in one corner, Cliff Richard in another. Me and Danny stood there with our whiskies: "What the fuck's going on?" It all got a bit easier as everyone got off their heads. We started to mingle. Radiohead introduced us to Cliff, telling him that we'd got a single out and I was only 18 . . . '

Misty-eyed with a mix of nostalgia and condescension, Cliff mused that he himself had released his first single at the tender age of 17.

'Yeah,' Gaz shot back, 'but I bet it wasn't about doing drugs.'

And did you or did you not cop off with Shampoo?

Gaz: *'Shampoo? We love 'em. We'd fuck 'em live on telly. No, I personally didn't.'*

Danny?

'I don't know. I honestly can't remember from midnight onwards.'

As Jimmy Pursey once put it: Tell Us The Truth.

'I've told you the fucking truth. I can't remember.'

That was Ronald Reagan's excuse. He's senile. You're 20.

'I lost touch with Danny about half-11,' recalls Gaz. 'I saw him again at two in the morning. I said, "What did you get up to?" He said, "I don't know. I just woke up in a hotel room with Sean Maguire, with Home And Away *stickers plastered all over me."'*

'I think I went somewhere with one of Shampoo,' concedes Danny.

Which one?

Danny's unblemished brow furrows in concentration.

'Um, the thinny.'

(From the pages of *Melody Maker*, February 11th, 1995)

PART THREE: SIMON BLACKMORE (PARLOPHONE PR)

SIMON Blackmore, Supergrass' current press agent, remembers the first time he met the band.

'They were wearing these mental *Starsky And Hutch* cardigans. They looked other-worldly. One of them had multi-coloured trousers on,' he told me. 'At the first Parlophone meeting there was a distinct smell of jazz cigarettes, which I thought was pretty cool.

'It soon became apparent that they had quite clearly defined ideas about what they were about and where they were going,' he continued. 'Which was great for me, cos obviously I'd heard the demo tape and knew they were destined for great things. To know that they had the self-belief to back it up was very heartwarming.

'Danny was hilarious, Gaz was cool, Mickey was sensible.'

'The first time I heard "Caught By The Fuzz",' Simon recalled, 'I just sat there and smiled all the way through. It was probably much like the time I came up to King's Reach Tower to play you the demo of "Mansize Rooster". And when I heard "Mansize Rooster", I laughed – I progressed from smiling to laughing in two songs, the tape was that good.'

(Ah yes. The playing of the demo of 'Mansize Rooster'. . . it had been a cold day, a dull day. We'd be playing our usual game of 'play it or break it' with a couple of dozen tapes, smashing the unlucky losers against a nearby wall or passing freelancer, whichever was nearer. Then Simon appeared, with a tape of the new Supergrass single. We knew Supergrass, we loved Supergrass. We'd played 'Caught By The Fuzz' way beyond death, driven everyone crazy with our bad Cockney pronunciations of that *'Ere comes my mum'* line. We wanted more 'Grass! We bundled into the Reviews Room, turned the volume to full. Within seconds, we were singing along. 'On the cover, NOW!', we howled. 'On the cover yesterday' . . .

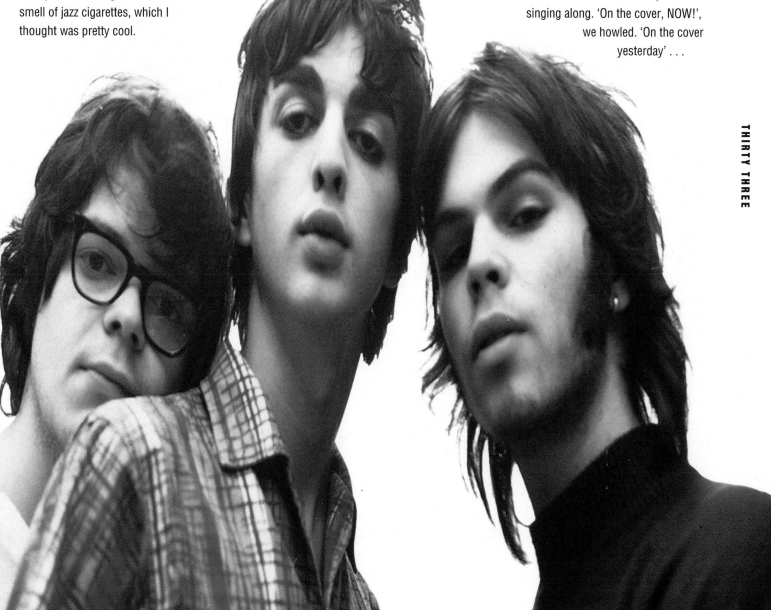

sorry. I digress again. Back to Simon.)

'Initially, I was worried that the band could have been just another New Wave Of New Wave act [a punk revivalist movement which Supergrass initially got lumped in with],' the PR explained, 'but when I heard the tape it was obvious it was something entirely different.'

I asked Simon to tell me about their Alexandra Palace gig (Supergrass played there in October '94, making their first major public appearance as support to Blur).

'I got to Alexandra Palace late, very pissed off,' he said. 'The band were doing a *Vox* interview at the bar, and they were getting strange looks from people, cos even then they looked like pop stars – even if you didn't know, you'd suspect. It was a lovely sunny day with a clear blue sky, and we sat and drank beer – although obviously not too much, as I was looking after them! The band went down tremendously, especially when they played 'Caught By The Fuzz' – even then it was obvious it would become a bit of an anthem.

'To the people who knew them, it was

clear Supergrass wouldn't be playing supports for very long. Alexandra Palace was like unleashing a best kept secret on an unsuspecting world.'

In the same month as they played the Palace, Supergrass supported their former mentors Ride at the Royal Albert Hall ('Two minutes before we went on stage, we were shitting ourselves,' Gaz told *Loaded* in November '94. 'In the end, it just felt like some journey up to heaven') and went out on their first major tour, as support to Shed Seven (where, on a couple of occasions, Gaz forgot the words to 'Caught By The Fuzz' !).

Already, the music press were starting to foam at the mouth.

'Respect due to tour support,' the *NME's* Simon Williams wrote in a review of their Edinburgh show. 'Supergrass zip through half-an-hour of power-crazed heroics with all the cocky self-assurance of teenage sensations who can sound like The Sex Pistols, Kingmaker and The Cardiacs in the same song, while taking NWONW [New Wave Of New Wave] to its natural, kinetic conclusion.'

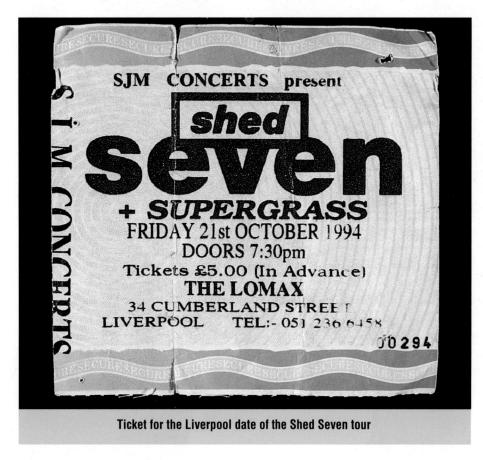

Ticket for the Liverpool date of the Shed Seven tour

INTERRUPTION THREE

WHAT is pop? Ah, I'm glad you're still paying attention. It's the tingle in your feet after a particularly satisfying orgasm; the way the phone rings off just as you reach it. It's the crumpling of a blue satin shirt; the teasing of a couple of stray hairs.

Let's get specific.

'"Caught By the Fuzz" is 150 seconds of pure fun, wherein a tale is related of being

On stage at Leeds during the Shed Seven trek

*caught on the "blow" by the cops and having to be bailed out by yer mum, who, you'd best believe, is none too pleased. Kinda like Shampoo's "Trouble" crossed with "Minder", if you will – and a possible outside bet for a November Number One. The song is raced through, all breathy denials and shouted accusations, like some-*thing very early Eighties and shameless.

'You'll play it 28 times (the acoustic version more than the electric), lose it down the back of the sofa, and, in five year's time, find it again and have a momentary ball playing Spot That Tune.'

(*MM* Single Of The Week, October 22, 1994. Reviewer: myself)

ADDENDA (1)

HERE is the story of the drug bust which was the inspiration for 'Caught By The Fuzz' .

When Gaz was 15, he and some mates were out cruising in a dodgy old motor, when some cops flagged them down. They had a dodgy tail light or something. Gaz was holding, so he stuffed the gear down the

front of his trousers . . . overlooking the fact he was wearing boxer shorts. So anyway, while he was being questioned by the law, the tin slid down the front of his pants and out onto the pavement. Oops.

The cops took Gaz down the station for a grilling, and he was dead worried they would call his mum. So they gave him 15 minutes to try to think of someone else he could call (perhaps his brother? – *'If only my brother could be here now/He'd get me out and sort me out alright'*), but in the end he had to get her in, and as you might imagine, she wasn't best pleased.

Hence, the song.

ADDENDA (2)

'CAUGHT By The Fuzz' came out three times.

(i) On Backbeat, in August '94. While all the negotiations with Parlophone were going down, local music fan Dave Norland put out the demo version of 'Caught By The Fuzz' b/w 'Strange Ones' as a 1,000 limited edition seven-inch (no picture sleeve) on his own Oxford label. Dave was an enthusiast, a fan of the band, who – possessing no phone – would meet up with Supergrass in a nearby pub and talk to them there. Parlophone agreed to the deal, feeling that it would help create just the right sort of 'grass roots' buzz. The single was sold at concerts and local record stores.

On the beach at Port Merion, North Wales, while shooting the 'Alright' video

'"Caught By The Fuzz" was deliberately undersold,' explains Simon Blackmore. 'The whole idea was that Supergrass should happen very organically, word-of-mouth, and with hindsight it worked.'

(As a curious postscript to this, 500 copies of the demo version of 'Mansize Rooster' were issued on the same label two months later. Although all parties seem unconcerned about it now, it was clear that both Parlophone and the band were annoyed at the time. 'I was fucked off with it, to be honest,' said Gaz, more worried about the fact it was the inferior demo version than any legal difficulties which might have arisen. 'It doesn't sound very good.')

(ii) On Fierce Panda, in September. *NME* journalist/Camden scenester Simon Williams heard the Backbeat single, and offered to include the demo on his label's 'Crazed & Confused' EP, alongside fellow teen sensations Credit To The Nation and Ash.

(iii) On Parlophone, in October.

It was made Single Of The Week in both national music papers, and ended up reaching Number 43 in the national charts with minimal promotion. The song was also voted into both *NME's* and *Melody Maker's* Critics Top 10 Singles Of The Year and into the top five of Radio 1FM DJ's John Peel's *Festive 50.*

By the end of 1994, it was apparent that Supergrass were well on their way . . . but weren't they worried that – being so young n'all – they might run into trouble at home for the way they continually shot their mouths off about sex and drugs (particularly acid: Danny claimed to have dropped acid at his parents' 25th Anniversary Party; in an early interview, Gaz joked that his mother had heard so much shit about him doing acid that she was going to disown him) . . ?

'Thing is,'Gaz told **Melody Maker's Taylor Parkes,** *'my mum's an ex-English teacher, so she's really strict and really liberal at the same time.'*

Mickey: *'And boy, can you fucking spell.'*

Danny: *'Yeah, but it's horrible when your mate's mum tells you off! Eurrgghhhh!'*

Gaz: *'But anyway, she's cool. When 'Caught By The Fuzz' came out, she was really proud. I overheard her telling one of her friends, playing her the pre-release tape: "Oh yes, this song's autobiographical, of course… listen out for the third verse, that's where I come in!" '*

★★★★★★★★★★☆☆☆☆☆☆★★★

'More Cock Than Doodle-Do'
Supergrass Go Top 20

Gaz signs a girl's breast . . . Danny disses an old schoolteacher . . . Mickey reckons God's living under his sink . . . Supergrass support The Bluetones on a nationwide tour . . . appear on *The Word* . . . release a limited edition Sub Pop single, 'Lose It' . . . and hit the Top 20 with 'Mansize Rooster' . . . plus, even more pop!

'I don't understand the New Glam tag at all'

MAN-SIZED

WHEN I was about 15, 16 I had to go to hospital to have my balls reduced. They were too large, I had difficulty getting my trousers on of a morning. The girls were disappointed. 'Come on,' they pleaded, 'give us one last go.' The nurse jerked me off straight for 48 hours, but it didn't help reduce the swelling, only exaggerated it. Finally, they decided to operate. I couldn't walk for days afterwards. Nurses would glance at me with tears in their eyes: 'That poor kid.'

There's no joy in having a mansize rooster before your time.

YOU'RE 'ON'!

SUPERGRASS began 1995 by supporting Gene at the London Astoria for an *NME* 'On For '95' showcase of new bands. The *NME's* reviewer was predictably enthusiastic.

'Supergrass play with a ferocity which aims to dispel for good any dark, facetious rumours of flash-in-the-pan exuberance and brat-pack vileness,' she wrote. 'For the first time in months, we see a band really young enough for it to be A Big Statement.'

The band also found themselves nominated for Best New Band at the paper's pointless Brat Awards.

(The Brat Awards were set up by the *NME* a few years back as an alternative to the industry's equally ridiculous Brit Awards. Nowadays, the nominees for both sets of awards are almost indistinguishable. For this, we have to thank 'Britpop' – a movement which covers any band UK-based and wielding a guitar, designed to appeal to the xenophobic tendencies of the British race. But I don't intend to waste space on fatuous media labels. Let's get back to Supergrass.)

'I really liked it at the Brat Awards,' Danny told the *NME* a few weeks later. 'At the party afterwards I was going around with Phil Daniels. We were talking to him about how

he should have shagged Leslie Ash when they were making "Quadrophenia", how he didn't get anywhere, and how gutted he was about it.'

Already, the band were keen to downplay the scope of their ambition and potential teen appeal – check this snippet from the *Maker* from February . . .

'I don't understand the New Glam tag at all,' grouches Gaz. *'There are a lot of ballady, Sixties-type, Beach Boys-style songs on our album. Stuff from different eras. We don't have a defined style.'*

Wouldn't you like to invent a musical movement?

'Yeah,' Danny says, *'but it's not the key thing.'*

'If it's going to happen, it'll happen.' Gaz switches into modesty mode. Bo-ring. *'But it'd be very pretentious and outrageously confident to claim anything for ourselves. We're not out to create a whole new style of music. We're aware we*

'. .and now, live at the Brighton Beach . . . Supergrass!'

could disappear overnight. You don't want to start thinking about it too much. It's easy to get drowned in the whole fucking fame bullshit. Let's not get sucked up into a fantasy world.'

No, let's. That's the whole point.

Pop, remember… it can be double-edged. It's about having your mother phone up at nine in the morning cos she's seen your ex on breakfast tv; being splashed across page three of the national music press cos you've fallen over drunk in the road; being pestered by girls to sign their bra straps ('I did some girl's breast, actually,' Gaz told Scotland's *Sun Zoom Spark*, 'and some bloke said, "I'll have great fun licking that off later, mate. Cheers." I think she was his girlfriend'); being caught pissing in a hotel corridor and denying it for months afterwards.

Er, the music. What motivates you?
'It's natural, man,' propounds Gaz.
Bo-ring!
'Something that we all want to do. Suck

it all in, whatever comes. Use the energy.'

People form bands for one of three reasons: sex, revenge or escapism. Which one's yours?

Gaz: *'The third one. It's a way out of washing dishes for the rest of my life.'*

Danny: *'The second. There are a certain few people who I would really like to see having their noses rubbed in our success. That bastard who dissed me when I was 12. That teacher who kept me in detention, seven days a week, for three weeks. If they could see me now. . .'*

Mickey: *'It's good fun to fucking play the Albert Hall, know what I mean?'*

Spot on, that man.

'There are no strange pretensions,' Gaz told *NME's* Simon Williams the same month. 'It's just unnecessary to do that many interviews. There's only a certain amount that people need to know about you – they don't need to know my favourite colour or what pants I wear.'

The band's seeming lack of willingness to accept the most basic premises of pop (favourite colours! 'which side do you dress on, sir?' 60ft guitar riffs! sideburns!) was most unseemly.

What it came down to, though, was a fear of typecasting – Supergrass didn't want to be seen as the male Shampoo ('a couple of giggly teenage girls obsessed with becoming pop stars,' was how Gaz disparagingly put it).

They knew that their potential lay far beyond just that.

THAT SINKING FEELING

IN February, to coincide with the release of their second single, 'Mansize Rooster' b/w 'Sitting Up Straight', Supergrass appeared on the cover of *Melody Maker*. It was their first national cover story. The single crashed into the Top 20 a week later.

The interview began like this . . .
'I think God's living under my sink.'
OK, so Mickey sees God in the

Gaz plugs in

Danny rolls up for the next gig

plumbing. At all of 24, Mickey is the oldest of Supergrass. Maybe he speaks with greater spiritual wisdom than Danny (20) or Gaz (18).

Gaz: 'I reckon He's a black geezer with dreads, a bit wasted.'

Danny: 'I think He's massive.'

Pass the champagne, lads.

Mickey gives Gaz a vigorous slapping for no apparent reason.

Can we have a go?

'Get your own band.'

However much sense the band may (or may not) have made after almost three hours of drinking beer and champagne and smoking blow, there was no disguising the fact that Supergrass had arrived.

Almost as if out of nowhere.

Of course, the support slots to Shed Seven, Blur and Ride couldn't have hurt, nor

the press shots of a half-naked band necking champagne recklessly back from the bottle, nor Danny's willingness to snog anything that moved . . . nor the fact the single itself (inspired by a character in *Never Ending Story*, or so Gaz informed local magazine *Curfew*) was a solidly sensational, sorted gem in a classic English style – revealing a lineage that stretched back through Madness, Wizzard, The Faces and The Who.

'Supergrass are hysterical, hysterically funny and quite terrifyingly talented,' wrote the *NME*, making it Single Of The Week. 'They should be modelling stack heels with green mohicans and three button mohair suits.'

Smash Hits gave the single four dots out of five, *Hot Press* dug it, while *Melody Maker* typically couldn't make its mind up, reviewing it twice. First time round, it was compared favourably to obscure popsters

Jellyfish (something to do with a 'plink-plonk' piano). The second review didn't even bother to mention the music, instead snickering smuttily about the title's supposed reference to Enormous Love Sausages.

The line the band fed their press office at Parlophone was that the title referred to a really big chicken. But the kids all knew it was really about an extremely large penis – Mickey's, probably.

The video featured the band romping around in a white room, much like the one for The Jam's 'Going Underground', and splashing naked in a bath full of blue champagne – very much *unlike* any Jam single. Gaz briefly got up in drag. Some people said he looked like Pauline from Eastenders, but my household all favoured the Seventies *Charlie's Angels* look.

The video was co-directed by Danny's

brother Nick, and an old schoolfriend from Oxford, Dominic Hawley.

The single reached Number 20.

Supergrass *had* arrived – with a bullet!

WORD UP!

THE same month, Supergrass made their first tv appearance, performing 'Mansize Rooster' live on *The Word*, with loads of swirling target symbols behind them. To celebrate, the band brought all their mates down from Oxford with them. There were plenty of legs and things flying through the air as they took the stage.

One particular blonde-haired friend had dropped a substantial amount of acid on the coach down, and you can see him clearly on the live transmission, standing screaming, with his hands in the air. Presenter Dani Behr introduced The 'Grass as New Mods, which made everyone cringe. But even though it was the first time the group had been on tv, they were very nonplussed by it all. Supergrass took it all in their stride.

Also present were grungers Live, smoochers Jade, former *Generation Game* cult figure Isla St Clair hosting a sex quiz, and a 'Hopeful' whose task it was to lick an old man's foot.

Backstage with The Bluetones

SUPERGRASS

plus special guests

THE bluetones

appearing at

LIVERPOOL LOMAX

Tuesday 14th February

Tickets: £5 (advance) B/O 0151 709 4321 or Probe or The Lomax

Mansize Rooster - The new single from Supergrass released 6th February

LITTLE CRED ROOSTERS

ALSO in February, Supergrass began their first headline tour of the UK, with The Bluetones in support on all dates (30, in all). Some critics were already hailing it 1995's equivalent of a joint Oasis/Blur tour.

Others were even less restrained – check my notes from Glasgow's King Tut's Wah-Wah Hut.

Jesus! What happened?!

They started with 'Strange Ones' (from the first single), a heady three-and-a-half-minute rush of youthful adrenalin and absurdly catchy choruses, which segued seamlessly into 'Sitting Up Straight' (from the second single), a fulsome two-and-a-half-minute rush of manic adrenalin and outrageously catchy choruses, which segued seamlessly into the hit, 'Mansize Rooster', a rampant two-and-a-half minute rush of unstoppable adrenalin and fuck-me-I-thought-it-was-impossible-to-write-

songs-this-catchy-any-more choruses, which segued seamlessly into 'Time', a slightly slower, more thoughtful threeminute rush of sweat-drenched adrenalin and deadpan-cool catchy choruses, which . . .

Actually, by around this point, I was thinking 'OK, very good, very clever, you bastard Supergrasses, throw away all your best songs at the start, put everything you've got into the first 15 minutes, there's no fucking way you're gonna follow that, who do you think you are, the bleedin' Jam or Undertones or someone?', when fuck me sideways and call me Colin if a two-note piano riff didn't start up and they didn't top ALL THAT with a song called 'Alright', a song so impossibly catchy and youthful and poptastic, it made everything before look positively moribund by comparison . . .

And then they played 'Caught By The

Backstage bubbly on the Bluetones tour

Fuzz' and the whole fucking world exploded.

Already, Gaz was being trailed by a group of female fans called the Gazettes who followed him everywhere.

How does he deal with them?

'He just tells them to fuck off.'

'COMEDY REMOVABLE SIDEBURNS'

AS if the excitement of going on a major UK tour and scoring a *Top 20* hit wasn't enough, in March *Vox* included 'Sitting Up Straight' on their cover-mounted tape of Radio 1FM sessions, and hipster US label Sub Pop released 'Lose It' b/w 'Caught By The Fuzz' (acoustic edit).

Lisa Paulon, UK label boss, was a major fan of the band – and what with the import of 'Caught By The Fuzz' doing so well on college radio, and in San Francisco, particularly – it didn't take long for her to convince her American bosses to make Supergrass the third in a line of limited edition singles by UK bands, following NWONW torch-bearers S*M*A*S*H and spiky popsters Elastica.

Predictably, *NME* made it Single Of The Week, writing that it was 'further evidence that Supergrass write the least complicated, most immediately available guitar music available in this country and are probably destined for the sort of fame that means

posters on walls, Supergrass pencil cases, and birthday cards with comedy removable sideburns for your loved one's entertainment.'

(Gaz's sideburns continued to be a source of fascination for fans and press alike. In Winchester, one lad turned up with carpet tiles stuck to the side of his face. Popular descriptions of Gaz included 'an extra from *Planet Of The Apes*' and 'the Werewolf Of Oxford'. The band were also nicknamed Toke That, on account of their recreational activities and teen appeal.)

The single sold out in a day, instantly topping the indie charts and reaching Number 75 nationally, despite only 2,500 copies being pressed.

★★★★★★★★★★★★★★★★★★

'Lenny Kravitz Sitting On The Toilet'
Supergrass Go Top 10

Supergrass visit Japan . . . they play Radio 1FM's *Sound City* week . . . visit the United States . . . frighten penguins and Mark Goodier indiscriminately . . . and drink loads of champagne . . . oh, and also release 'Lenny' which charges straight into the Top 10 . . . plus: pop – is it overrated?

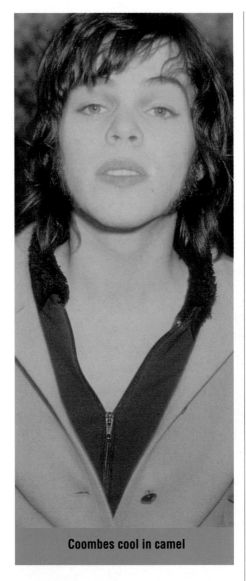

Coombes cool in camel

The mighty Quinn

Goffey . . . just groovy

FLY? SUPERFLY!

SUPERGRASS' intuitive understanding of POP was fast becoming second to none. Yet, oddly, all the signs they were giving off in interviews and on stage were those of unashamed rockers . . .

Gaz apologises for his voice being 'fucked'. Danny, not missing a beat, intones 'cocaine' in a deep New York accent. (Earlier, on the tour bus, the first word which comes out the speakers when the CD player is switched on is 'cocaine'. Spooky. Or perhaps not so when you consider this band listen to JJ Cale and the truly atrocious Frank Zappa's 'Dynamo Hum' for pleasure.)

Someone female yells, 'We fucking love you, Danny.'

A bare-chested Danny ('sorry about my

physique!') looks wildly round the crowd before crashing down full-force on his kit and kickstarting 'I'd Like To Know', which I've just decided is my new favourite song ever ever ever with its Bowie-esque line 'I'd like to go where all the strange ones go' . . . until, that is, they begin the mighty swirling bass riff to 'Lenny', which is like all the poppier sides of Led Zeppelin (if that ain't an oxymoron) rolled into three amphetamine-drenched minutes.

And what about the garage-y Sub Pop single 'Lose It', which is The Beatles' 'I Want To Hold Your Hand' in reverse – 'I won't come home 'cause you never hold my hand' – and their three-minute pummelling of Jimi Hendrix's 'Stone Free' as an encore?

Fucking wicked, man!

(From my notes on Supergrass' Edinburgh University show, March '95. The band's version of 'Stone Free' was later issued as a free seven-inch with vinyl copies of 'I Should Coco'.)

The fact that Supergrass knew their rock heritage was born out by their choice of records in *Melody Maker's* 'Rebellious Jukebox' feature; this is where bands are asked to name the dozen records which changed their lives.

Supergrass chose Gong, Sly And The Family Stone's 'Anthology' (Danny: 'It makes us feel like a million dollars'), The Beach Boys, Audio Active's dub reggae, David Bowie (Gaz used to be heavily into Ziggy Stardust), Jimi Hendrix, 'Revolver' (George is Gaz's favourite Beatle), Neil Young's classic 'After The Goldrush', Iggy Pop's 'Lust

For Life' and – for something slightly more up-to-date – Tricky.

'We don't know much about Tricky,' explained Danny. 'He comes from Bristol and I like Bristol because my brother lives there and he sees Tricky walking around, so I feel quite close to him!'

…And not one mention of Madness or Blur among them.

SO WHAT IS POP?

HELL. There's nothing wrong with *subtlety*.

Supergrass are allowed their heritage. It helps lend their songs a certain ease, a grace that is all the more beguiling cos it appears so effortless. Without this knowledge, the joins, the cracks, would be much more apparent. Who cares what the future will bring? We're concerned with the NOW. Supergrass ain't mindlessly reverential, anyhow. They *plunder*.

And, in case you're still wondering, here's the difference between Supergrass and the other young British contenders . . .

In a recent *Melody Maker* interview, one of Menswear excused the awfulness of his band's debut album, remarking that it took The Beatles 'God knows how long to get to "Sgt Pepper"'.

'Sergeant Pepper's Lonely Hearts Club Band' is actually The Beatles' *worst* album.

AMERICAN PIE

IN April, shortly after they played Bristol's Anson Rooms as part of Radio 1FM's 'Sound City' week (and by popular opinion blew headliners EMF off the stage), Supergrass were interviewed for their first *NME* cover story on the eve of their first visit to America. Ted Kessler's heavily impressionistic feature dwelt on Supergrass' history, pre-trip nerves and the band's chemistry…

Danny's older, but Gaz is more mature. Danny's out there, open to new experiences and willing to get into trouble to gain knowledge. He fancies maybe living abroad in a couple of years and making some experimental, laidback music.

'I'd rather be JJ Cale than in Blur, y'know. Being a pop group's fine, but there's

more to us than that. We're artists, too.'

Gaz, on the other hand, has swallowed the rock'n'roll work ethic and plans to make at least six albums with Supergrass. Gaz thinks that in the end Mickey will always bind them together.

'We're like scales, I suppose. Danny's at one end with his head in the clouds, always trying to leap off into new experiences, while Mickey's at the other end with his feet on the ground, putting things into perspective. And I'm in the middle, saying hello to both of them.'

In the bandroom, Sound City, Bristol

The two-week promotional trip to the States (where they were signed to Capitol) was relatively restrained. Although they did manage to get into trouble on the flight over…

'We were just really drunk,' Danny told *Vox*. 'We'd had loads of champagne and I asked the stewardess if I could meet the pilot. Our sound engineer kept asking which button made the plane go faster. They were really scared of us for some reason . . .'

The *NME* review from Washington DC, where they supported the rampant Rhode Island rock band Scarce, reported how impressively they held the small crowd's attention – 'Then again, who wouldn't be swayed by The Jam-meets-Sweet singalong

"Strange Ones", the swish and swagger of "Time", the back alley glam-strut "Odd?", or any of the other dozen tunes?' the awestruck US reporter asked.

'The first thing we saw in LA was this woman with silicone tits up to her chin,' babbled Danny to *Vox's* Stephen Dalton in July. 'And the first person we met at the hotel was Harvey from *Cagney And Lacey*. We asked if he wanted to join us in the jacuzzi, but he had some adverts to do . . .'

'We were told there was a buzz, especially in LA,' said Gaz, 'but the plan wasn't to go over and conquer America. We were just meeting people we were going to be working with at Capitol.'

'It's a really fucked-up country,' Danny finally decided. 'Everyone's on drugs, or they seem to be.'

TURNING JAPANESE

IN April, Supergrass also visited Japan, just to visit their record company, where they got their first taste of the legendary Japanese female rock fan.

'We've just got back from Japan,' Gaz told MM's Taylor Parkes in his May interview, 'and that was fucking weird. They all wait outside the hotel, and then

when we come out and get in a taxi to go to, say, the EMI building, they all get in taxis and follow us, then wait outside the EMI building.'

Mickey: *'They're all so polite as well, even when they try to chat you up.'*

Gaz: *'They say, "Maybe later, you and me, we might be able to go out together tonight, if you would like that."'*

Danny: *'It's really good fun to frighten them by hiding round corners, then jumping out and going "RAAAAARRRRGGGGHHHHHH!!!"'*

remarked upon its similarity to Led Zeppelin, circa 'Physical Graffiti'. *Vox*, being marginally older, compared it to The Who and The Cream.

Even the indie *Hello!, Select*, got in on the act, making it Single Of The Month.

The video, shot by Nick and Dom once more, was filmed on the band's just-completed US tour, in LA's Dragonfly Club. It featured a girl dancing in a green jumper at what was supposed to be her first gig, maybe freaking out on a concoction of drugs

'We wanted a real Led Zeppelin feel to it,' Gaz explained. 'I'm a big fan of theirs'.

houses are made out of cardboard – the Queen Vic, Albert Square, the cafes, everything. The band toyed with the idea of swapping their photo for Debbie's on the sideboard in Nigel's living room, but then we heard rustlings, so we scarpered. Lili Wilde, the photographer, shot them in the bushes, and the band were making fun of her leather gear, asking if she had any bondage gear on her… you should have seen their faces when she pulled a pair of handcuffs out of her bag!'

'All in all, a top day out.'

So, Top Of The Pops, *then.*

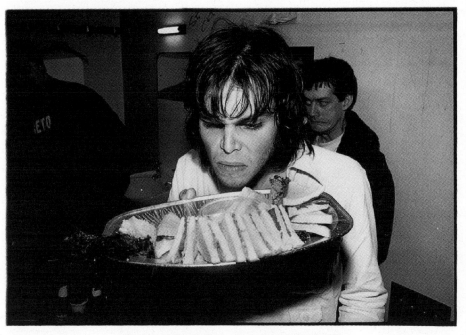

'How long have these been hangin' round?'

Shagged out, Bristol

'SMUG-LOOKING PENGUINS'

SUPERGRASS' new single, 'Lenny' b/w 'Wait For The Sun' was released on May 1st. Initial quantities of the seven-inch came on sky-blue vinyl, with some rather smug-looking penguins on the sleeve, courtesy of the ace Supergrass sleeve designers from Oxford known as Moody Painters. According to Gaz, this single was 'about running away from your troubles'.

By now, the critical plaudits were coming in thick and fast.

Melody Maker made it Single Of The Week, enthusing that it was 'effortless, upbeat, young and boisterous'. *NME* referred to its 'genital-rumbling magnificence' and

EAST END BOYS

'LENNY' was the first time Supergrass per-formed on *Top Of The Pops*. The band's press agent Simon Blackmore takes up the story…

'"Lenny" opened the show,' he recalls. 'It sounded very rocky, and they jumped up and down a lot – they were on a bit of a high, after going straight into the *Top 10*. Old tour-mates Shed Seven were on the show too, and kept interrupting Taylor Parkes' interview for *Melody Maker* to ask if Supergrass wanted to play football. And Celine Dion was wandering up and down the corridor, practising her high notes – everyone was yelling at her to shut up.

'We sneaked onto the *Eastenders* set at the back of Elstree Studios, where all the

Feel like pop stars yet?

Gaz: *'I did a minute ago, cos you just gave me a drink for no money.'*

Danny: *'It's just life, man.'*

(From the *Melody Maker* cover feature, 20th May, 1995)

BABYSITTERS ON ACID

AS ever, the band were remarkably laidback about their success, as DJ Mark Goodier found out to his cost when he attempted to interview Danny over the telephone for Radio 1FM's *Top 40* show.

'And now we go over to Danny from top indie band Supergrass! Danny, hi!' Danny, who was babysitting at the time, picked up

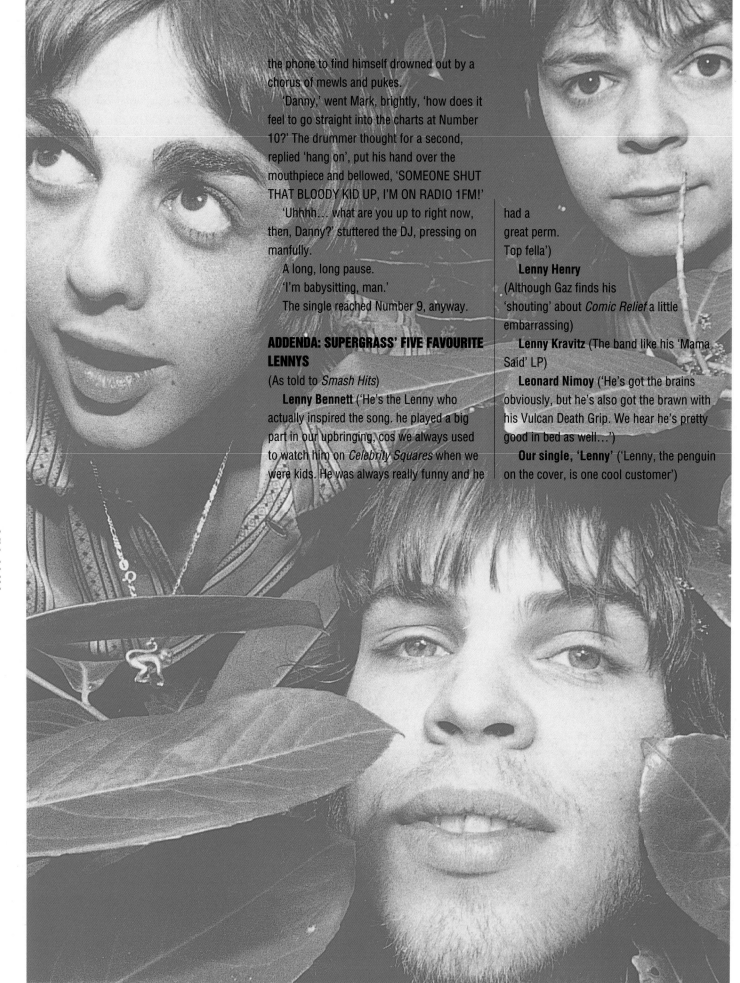

the phone to find himself drowned out by a chorus of mewls and pukes.

'Danny,' went Mark, brightly, 'how does it feel to go straight into the charts at Number 10?' The drummer thought for a second, replied 'hang on', put his hand over the mouthpiece and bellowed, 'SOMEONE SHUT THAT BLOODY KID UP, I'M ON RADIO 1FM!'

'Uhhhh… what are you up to right now, then, Danny?' stuttered the DJ, pressing on manfully.

A long, long pause.

'I'm babysitting, man.'

The single reached Number 9, anyway.

ADDENDA: SUPERGRASS' FIVE FAVOURITE LENNYS

(As told to *Smash Hits*)

Lenny Bennett ('He's the Lenny who actually inspired the song. he played a big part in our upbringing, cos we always used to watch him on *Celebrity Squares* when we were kids. He was always really funny and he had a great perm. Top fella')

Lenny Henry (Although Gaz finds his 'shouting' about *Comic Relief* a little embarrassing)

Lenny Kravitz (The band like his 'Mama Said' LP)

Leonard Nimoy ('He's got the brains obviously, but he's also got the brawn with his Vulcan Death Grip. We hear he's pretty good in bed as well…')

Our single, 'Lenny' ('Lenny, the penguin on the cover, is one cool customer')

★★★★★★★★★★★★★★★★★

'You're Kidding Me!'
Supergrass Hit Number One

Supergrass' 'I Should Coco' makes a stunning Number One debut LP . . . producer Sam Williams describes its recording . . . Gaz gives a track-by-track rundown . . . plus loads of quotes from magazines each trying to out-do the other in singing the album's praises . . . also: pop – is it just a Batman mug, or is it an MN8 setlist?

COCO POPPED!

WORK on Supergrass' debut album 'I Should Coco' began in February 1994 (before the band were even signed to Parlophone!) when the lads went down to Cornwall with producer Sam Williams. The songs recorded during that session ('Caught By The Fuzz', 'Mansize Rooster', 'Sitting Up Straight', *et al*) ended up 15 months later on the LP in pretty much their original form – give or take a few overdubs, paper'n'comb ensembles and vocal retakes.

The bulk of the album was recorded shortly after the group exchanged contracts with their label, July 5-21, the same year.

'The record company gave us 500 quid as a float to get us down to the studio [Sawmills] in a van,' Sam recalled in *Melody Maker*, 'and most of that was gone in about half-an-hour before we left Oxford on various substances to keep the session going. It was really lovely weather for about half of the time – the first week it pissed down with rain and we got loads of recording done. We

Supergrass, pinball wizards

Under the blue sky, I should coco

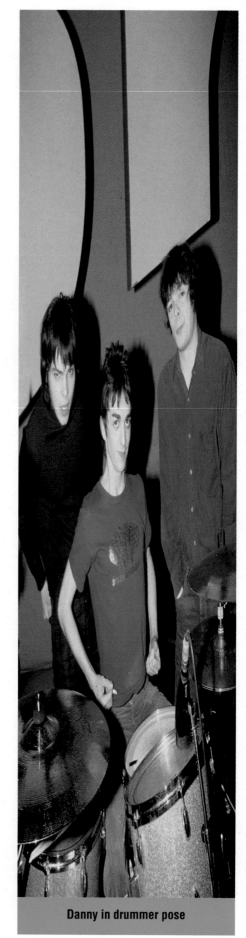

Danny in drummer pose

recorded all the backing tracks in four days or something.'

The harmonies were done through cheap mics which were then put through little guitar effects pedals, to get the sound as trashy and distorted as possible. Sometimes, though, the band's copious use of 'blow' would affect the vocals and Gaz would receive a stern warning to go a little easier . . . which he'd invariably ignore, sneaking upstairs for a crafty smoke when he thought no one was looking.

'About halfway through,' Sam continued, 'we'd done all the tracks and I thought we'd probably have the album finished by the end of the second week. Then it came time to do some vocals, and I was rubbing my hands saying 'OK right, let's finish the record', and suddenly they all went, 'Well, actually, we haven't got any lyrics for most of the songs', which was really funny. We ended up just busking through a few things that they did have some words for.'

After finally coming up with the appropriate lyrics, the mixing took place in December – 'I Should Coco' being completed the following February, when the last few overdubs to 'Sofa (Of My Lethargy)' were added.

Even before Supergrass had hit the Top 40, they had the material primed and ready to storm the barricades.

WHAT IS POP? (REPRISE)

YOU must be getting the idea by now.

Instinct. Bewilderment. The knowledge that if you don't grab the moment another one'll be along any second. The ability to crow 'You should have been there', whether the other person should've or not. Enthusiasm. Sequins. Tiny stick-on hearts which fall off at the slightest provocation. Fake leopardskin circles plastered on sticky walls. Words spelt out on love-heart ringlets. Xeroxed pages of hastily-scribbled opinions. Supergrass' song 'Sex!' (originally released as the third track on the CD of 'Lenny'), which is like Jim Bowen taking Anna Friel down the country path for a lesson in semantics. Batman mugs. MN8 set lists. Anything which retains its core of pleasure,

On the road, in a caff, life goes on . . .

which sticks silver lines over gaping mouths.

What is pop? It's the trembling you feel in the pit of your stomach, queuing to get into the tent at Supergrass' T In The Park performance, scared that you might miss just one precious moment. It's the agitation you suffer running for the last train after Supergrass' London Astoria 2 show, knowing that you'd already seen that song *15 fuckin' times already*. It's, oh . . .

'Stupendous, exhilarating, dazzling, shocking, startling, first-class, genuine, bona-fide SUPERGRASS!, diverse, skilled, stimulating, engaging, Jesus-H-Christ,

MAKING TRACKS

IN April '95, Gaz gave the *Melody Maker's* News Desk an exclusive track-by-track rundown of the LP.

'The title is kind of taking the piss out of all this Cockney bullshit,' he explained. 'It's like, "Supergrass — I should coco. If you believe them, you'll believe anything."'

'I'd Like To Know': 'There's a lot of freaky people that we've met over the last two years, and that's generally what it's about. There are guys in Oxford that you see walking around town all the time, doing the same thing — like the Paper Man, who always

Fuzz' and then they thought that 'Mansize Rooster' was more of an experiment and like an extension of what we'd done before. Actually, they're both from the same batch.'

'Alright': 'A real summer track.'

('We redid the piano on 'Alright' because it wasn't out-of-tune enough,' Sam Williams told *MM's* Control Zone. 'They'd done the demo of it on Danny's mum's upright, which is a really fucked-up old house piano, and they wanted to get that sound. So I just detuned the grand at Sawmills, detuning a string on every second note within the two octave range they were using. It sounded

Danny in barefoot action during the American tour, September '95

glorious . . . er . . . good. The type of record that you treasure for life, [that you] apply anti-static fluid to every night, kiss, caress, basically adore . . . '

(From *Mansize Fanzine's* review of 'I Should Coco'.)

What is pop? Infatuation. Desire. Love. Stupidity.

Gaz: *'The most embarrassing moment in pop is on our album where it goes, "Oi Mum! Got any mandies?"'*

Mickey: *'Yeah, that gets on my tits too! Why the hell did we put that on?'*

walks around with masses of newspapers sticking out of every pocket and big bundles under every arm. In America, we kept getting accosted for more and more money — $10, $15, rising all the time. And if you give them a couple of bucks then it's, 'What about your friends, man, have your friends got any money?' You really freak out.'

'Caught By The Fuzz'/'Mansize Rooster': 'They're both really early songs, and they were written within a week of each other, although they sound quite different. Lots of people's first taste of us was 'Caught By The

perfect because it had this slightly haphazard thing about the tuning. We just tried to get it as pubby as we could without wrecking the piano too much.')

'Lose It': 'The whole vibe was 'Let's freak out on this one' which is why the vocals come across the way they do, with those repeated lines *'Don't lose it/I won't come home/'Cause you never hold my hand'*. It's quite an angry song about being spoiled.'

'Lenny': 'I saw the video for this the first time last night and it looked really good — really dark, seedy and dirty.'

'Strange Ones': 'Originally, we imagined it having a kind of Dexy's Midnight Runners feeling, but we ended up turning what was going to be the brass line into a vocal line.'

'Sitting Up Straight': 'That's one of my favourites on the album. I think it should undoubtedly have been a single instead of "Mansize Rooster".'

'She's So Loose': 'It's about being young and going to a pub, meeting some strange girl and ending up having a night of crazed passion with someone you hardly know! It's about someone who's really upfront. Like the American girls – not that I'd know, but just

night and just picked up a guitar and started playing this bluesy kind of shit. We're all real blues fans – Hendrix is a big hit with us.'

'Sofa (Of My Lethargy)': 'That was a jam in the studio. We were out in Cornwall by this estuary and it was a beautiful day. We had a nice smoke and got into the vibe. I set up the piano, there was a Hammond, we all got on separate instruments and then the engineer just pressed "record".'

'I don't think it's the sort of music you could masturbate to,' Danny remarked thoughtfully to MM's *Taylor Parkes.*

'But you could have sex to it,

we've given the album a good start with something like 'I'd Like To Know', progressed through a lot of different weird shit and then ended with a song like that.'

WHAT IS POP? (REPRISE)
SEE above.

If I wanted to come over all clever and sociological and stuff, I could claim that the line *'Sleep around/If we like'* from 'Alright' heralds a sea-change in the post-AIDS consciousness of the younger generation, indicates that finally a new generation is reacting against the 'safe sex' generation of

Danny it says and Danny it is

from observing!'

'We're Not Supposed To': 'It kind of sums up a part of how we are with each other. It's kind of about when you're in your early teens, and you get your mum and your teachers going, "You're not supposed to do that, you know".'

('The words are a bit dodgy,' Mickey told *Vox* in March. 'You can read it as a paedophilia song that sounds a little bit like "The Laughing Gnome".')

'Time': 'That came from one night when I got home really fucked off after a really shit

definitely,' responded Gaz.

'Yeah, but you could have sex to . . . fuckin' monks, or something,' exploded Danny.

'You could definitely have sex to 'Sofa (Of My Lethargy)',' the singer continued. *'Real nice smooth sex. It only lasts six minutes? Well, without foreplay, obviously.'*

'Time To Go': 'Another really old one that we originally did on four-track in my room. It didn't take long in the studio, and it really works well in that context. It's good that

the Eighties, in much the same way as the Seventies 'squares' reacted against the promiscuity of the Sixties hippies. But I don't. So I won't. Anyhow, nowhere in 'Alright' does it state whether it is, or isn't, cool to use condoms, although one might imagine that pure commonsense – plus an instinctive desire to keep on feeling *'alright'* – indicates that the former's the case.

Supergrass sleep around. If they like.

It's that simple.

It's that stupid.

As stupid as . . . pop.

'Breathless, brash and bumptious . . .'

WATER SPORTS

'I SHOULD Coco' was released on May 9th, 1995, to both instant commercial success and critical acclaim.

It charted at Number 3, hung around in the Top 40 and – in the wake of the tremendous success of the 'Alright' single and Channel 4's Glastonbury coverage (where Supergrass starred) – hit the top spot 10 weeks later, despite stiff competition from the much-hyped Michael Jackson comeback album. It stayed there three weeks, finally being toppled by Black Grape's debut ' It's Great When You're Straight . . . Yeah', in the process becoming the first debut LP by a band on Parlophone to go platinum since The Beatles' 'Please, Please Me', over three decades earlier.

At the time of writing, it's still in the Top 40, 23 weeks on – 'It sure ain't Sleeper,' as one industry insider succinctly put it.

To celebrate the album reaching Number One, Supergrass were invited to perform live from Vancouver, Canada for *Top Of The Pops*. In a scene reminiscent of Blondie's classic 'Union City Blue' video, the group set up their equipment on the side of some docks, before racing through a very punky version of 'Caught By The Fuzz'. Danny, who was suffering from a very bad hangover, ran down over the edge to the water before the last beat was even played.

The drummer claimed in *Q*, a trifle unconvincingly, that he was 'actually a little sad at knocking Jon Bon Jovi off the top.

'He puts in a lot of work and he's a good icon for teenagers,' Danny added sarcastically. 'Michael Jackson – well, he tried hard too.'

Without question, Supergrass had MOST DEFINITELY arrived.

WHAT IS POP? (FINAL REPRISE)

FROM Parlophone's press office's cuttings library, re: 'I Should Coco'.

Time Out: 'The first remarkable thing you notice about 'I Should Coco', the debut album from Supergrass, is that it lasts for 40 minutes yet sounds like it was recorded in 35. The second thing you notice is how ace it is.'

In concert at Le Palais, Hammersmith

NME (9/10): 'Like bathing in sunlight. They've got it all and they know it. Nothing can touch them.'

Melody Maker (recommended): 'Debauchery is fun, and fun is good for you, and there is no moral distinction between picnicking in the park, skinning up on the bus and sleeping around if you feel like it.'

Mojo: 'Like a nude Noddy Holder starting a fight.'

Vox (8/10): 'A rude-kid splash of pop-punk that shows up every other tip for the top as the po-faced, serious-muso, thoroughly adult, business ventures they undoubtedly are.'

Encore (14/15): 'Have fun, enjoy. Incidentally, "I Should Coco" was Reg Varney's catchphrase in *On The Buses*.'

Q (4/5): 'Everything that might make them great is here, albeit in kit form.'

Select (3/5): 'One of those debuts that scoffs at patronising comments like "promising".'

Hot Press (10/12): 'Everything that teenage should be – getting drunk, getting stoned, getting laid, getting into trouble and NOT getting old.'

Sun Zoom Spark: 'It's OK to have a good time.'

Daily Telegraph: 'It won't change the face of pop music, but it is utterly infectious.'

The Times: 'Breathless, brash and bumptious, but only in a way that would not cause your granny undue concern.'

The Guardian (5/5): 'Album of the year stuff.'

BRITPOP. PLEASE STOP

THE critic from *Q* (the rock magazine for pensioners) claimed that it was self-evident Supergrass were only successful because of some supposed resurgence in British music (the 'Britpop' syndrome).

The band, however, weren't having any of it.

'Does it have anything to do with British pop?' Gaz asked, affronted. 'Isn't it just something to do with Supergrass having made a good album? I don't feel part of a Britpop scene. I don't feel any association with the other bands, even though I like some of them. I like The Bluetones and The Nubiles and The Mystics. I mean, Elastica, Echobelly, Menswear… no offence, lovely people, but we're nothing to do with that.

'The bloke from Menswear came up to me and said, straight-faced "Gaz, let's bond",' the singer added. 'He was desperate to know what I thought of his band. He's a nice bloke but why should I want to bond with Menswear.'

Exactly.

Pop is Supergrass is pop… not pop is Supergrass is part-of-some bleedin' -larger-overall-revivalist- movement-that-by-definition -cuts-out-anyone-who-isn't- white-and-is-designed-to-give- us-back-'our'-pride-in-a-notion-of- 'nationality'-which-went-out-in-the- Fifties-along-with-National-Service… is pop.

Pop is Supergrass IS pop. Full stop.

★★★★★★★☆☆☆☆★★★★★★★

'Smoke A Fag, Put It Out'
Supergrass Feel 'Alright'

'Smoke A Fag, Put It Out'

They land at Glastonbury in a helicopter . . . Danny appears on *Melody Maker*'s 'Shelter' cover . . . they release 'Alright', as the whole country goes feelgood mad . . single Number 2 . . . pop: sticking two fingers up to authority

The band relax . . .   **. . . before they triumph . . .**   **. . . at Glastonbury**

GOLDEN SHOWER

IN May, Supergrass set out on a short headline tour of the UK, including dates at Manchester Hacienda, Glasgow Plaza and Hammersmith Palais. Meanwhile, 'Odd?' (the extra track on the CD of 'Mansize Rooster') was reissued on the Fierce Panda compilation LP 'Nings Of Desire', alongside The Bluetones, Gorky's Zygotic Mynci and The Weekenders (the track also turned up later in the year on *Melody Maker's* 'Hold On' Samaritans benefit compilation CD).

'Dreams are excellent,' enthuses Mickey. 'I write songs in dreams, songs like 'Odd?'. It's based around drowning in the sea.'

'I remember pissing in the wardrobe once when I was asleep,' Danny adds. 'Going into my brother's room, opening the wardrobe door and just pissing into it.'

Mickey: *'I knew this bloke in Brighton who used to stand up in the middle of the night and piss all over his girlfriend in his sleep.'*

Did she chuck him?

'No, she was really into it.'

(From *Melody Maker*, 2/95)

UNFEASIBLY LARGE CHOPPER

THE following month, Supergrass played their first summer festival – at Glastonbury, where they turned up in a helicopter laid on for them by the *NME*. Despite the considerable expense thus incurred, the paper still put Rolling Stone Keith Richards on the cover instead of Supergrass – an irony which probably didn't escape the group, being such ardent lovers of classic rock. 'Out with the new, in with the old,' one might almost say.

Although it was Supergrass' first appearance at a festival as a band, they'd been to plenty as punters.

'I was at the Castlemorton rave,' Danny told the *NME's* Keith Cameron on the way to the site (Danny used to be a confirmed raver). 'That was mental. There were about 30,000 people there, the last illegal rave. I don't know if this will be as exciting. It'll be extremely hard to stay straight here, though.'

Keith's feature waxed rhapsodically about the band's nerves at getting into the helicopter, the chopper's pilot ('the last band

The only way to travel for up and coming superstars . . .

we carried was ZZ Top'), strange sub-breeds of festival-goers . . .'. before revealing that everyone thought the ride was great fun – 'just like being on a rollercoaster'.

'Mickey's month-old baby [Daisy], and his girlfriend were at Glastonbury,' Simon Blackmore, the band's press agent, recalled. 'It was all very communal with the bus backstage, everybody was camped there for the day – except for Danny of course, who

disappeared within five minutes and came back wearing a purple'n'green sequinned tea-cosy hat, yellow shades and eating Zen noodles just before the band were due on.'

For their performance, the band walked on stage wearing spoof Stone Roses masks (the Roses had been expected to make their long-awaited UK return headlining Glastonbury, but an injury to guitarist John Squire's arm forced the band to pull out),

going 'Ey! We fookin' made it in the end!' in fake Northern accents.

Gaz burbled something about Crosby, Stills & Nash, the crowd went mental pogoing during 'Alright', and the set finished on 'Lenny', as ever. Another triumph!

'We're all horrible pessimists,' Mickey remarked to Keith Cameron afterwards, sipping Red Bull under the misapprehension it was beer. 'What can go wrong will go

. . . Supergrass take the *NME* helicopter from Glastonbury

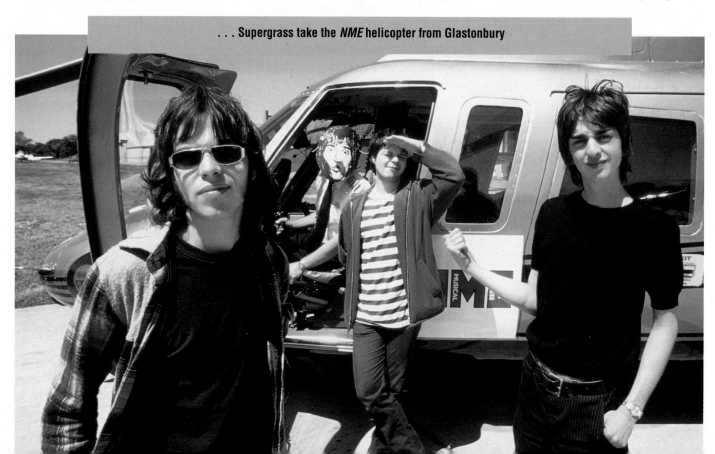

wrong in our heads, when actually it's going alright. You know you're still up there with your two best mates. Walking up to Danny and looking at him and having him laugh at you. It's not like playing a gig, cos you look at people at gigs, pick them out and play songs to them. All you can see here is people's arms waving. It's something we're not used to.'

And with that, the band departed.

(Supergrass were in the middle of a European tour, during which they played at the Roskilde festival, where Oasis and The Cure both visited them backstage – Oasis saying something like 'You're the fookin' future of rock'n'roll, you are', while Robert Smith insisted on trying to teach Gaz the 'proper' way to play 'Stone Free'.)

CRIMINAL IN-JUSTICE

IN July, 'Lose It' was reissued by Sub Pop as part of their 'Helter Shelter' box set in aid of the homeless charity, Shelter. To help publicise the event, *Melody Maker* put Danny on its cover, alongside Ed S*M*A*S*H, Justin, the drummer from Elastica, and Steve Mason of Gene – the three other bands involved. A cover-mounted cassette, featuring 'Sitting Up Straight', also appeared.

Danny donned a garish gold shirt for the occasion, and proceeded to do the exact opposite of whatever the photographer asked. And as to why he was there? He seemed genially perplexed, but, as he explained to *The Maker's* Ian Gittins, he did sometimes give money to homeless people in the street.

'Yeah, well, I might as well,' the drummer shrugged, 'because I'd only spend it on fags and beer otherwise. I get caught out sometimes, though. I gave two quid a couple of weeks ago to this guy who was sitting on a bench looking really fucked. He seemed a bit surprised. I walked off, then I turned round and I saw him get up, get into his car and drive off!'

Ian asked Danny whether Supergrass had played any benefit gigs. (After all, their songs could hardly be said to deal with socio-political issues.)

Mickey crunching crisps

STRANGE ONES
SITTING UP.
MAN SIZE
TIME
I'D LIKE TO KNOW.
SHE'S SO LOOSE
FUZZ
LENNY

'Nah, they're all us-against-the-world songs,' he replied. 'Oh, we played a few benefits in Oxford when we were called The Jennifers. We played one gig for the Criminal Justice Bill.'

– Don't you mean *against* it?

– 'Yeah, *against* it.'

The four bands were also scheduled to play a concert for Shelter, the charity for the homeless, but unfortunately Supergrass were in Japan at the time, so instead – in answer to a plea from Ride's Laurence Colbert – they played an over-heated secret gig at the 1,000 capacity Abingdon Old Jail in Oxford, with Echobelly and The Candyskins

in support, in aid of the Key Issue appeal.

Danny had to leave the stage a few times, though…

'The 'Grass are halfway through their set, having played 'Fuzz', 'Mansize Rooster', 'Odd?', etc, when Danny, now visibly suffering, stumbles off stage in search of some oxygen. The crowd also feeling the heat, seem distressed and impatient for the return of the drumming dynamo, and after several calls for calm from Gaz and Mickey who stand awkwardly on stage, Danny reappears and booms into the microphone, "I'm dying… I'm dying…"

'They manage a few more numbers, including an excellent version of "She's So Loose" before leaving the stage, for what, if Danny could have had his way, would have been the last time. Somehow, however, he manages to summon up the energy to come back and play "Lenny" their usual encore, at which point, Barney [from Supergrass designers, The Moody Painters] starts screaming "I drew the penguin" over and over again…'

(From *Mansize Fanzine 2* – see address at the back of this book)

SHADDAP YOUR FACE

ON July 3rd, Parlophone released Supergrass' first double A-side and fourth single, 'Alright'/'Time', on orange vinyl. The music press, as ever, were more than enthusiastic . . .

Terrorvision made it Single Of The Month in *Select*; *NME* claimed that it 'staple-guns its grinning self to your memory' while giving it their obligatory Single Of The Week; it merited five blobs out of five in *Smash Hits*; *The Guardian* called 'Alright' the year's 'most ridiculously carefree musical moment'; *Top Of The Pops* magazine termed it 'excellent'; *MM* boasted that Supergrass were 'pretty cool at turning the bleeding obvious into the intangibly loveable', while comparing it to The Rutles' genius Beatles spoof 'I Must Be In Love'; and *Music Week*, rather patronisingly, said it was 'an anthem for the younger generation'.

Daily Sport topped the lot however, when they claimed that the band were as surprised as anyone else at the single's success . . . Danny was supposed to have been upstairs with a girl when the news broke, and was alleged to have stammered, 'I can't believe it! We've gone straight in at Number 2 and I was just upstairs straight in at Number 69!'

The video to 'Alright' was shot in Portmeirion, a village on the coast of Northwest Wales, where cult Sixties tv show, *The Prisoner* was filmed. Danny looked as if he'd been dressed in the top half of Chewbacca's cast-offs, while Gaz was sporting a pair of luminous hipsters.

According to a script 'liberated' by *Loaded* magazine, it was supposed to reflect the 'feel alright' vibe of the song and contain subtle references ranging from *The Prisoner* (a big white ball chasing the boys) to *The Monkees* (speeded-up gags) to *Bedknobs And Broomsticks* (a massive travelling bed) to *Double Deckers* (riding Chopper bikes).

This it did, spectacularly well.

'We want it to be like those early Beatles films, *Help* and that lot,' Gaz told *Loaded*. 'I like it when they just fuck around and don't give a shit about looking cool.'

Spot on, that man.

'THAT NAGGING PIANO'

I ASKED Supergrass' PR, Simon Blackmore, to tell me about the first time he heard 'Alright'.

'There was just . . . that piano, that nagging piano,' he replied. 'I couldn't get it out of my head for days. Then there was all those things about lighting fags and brushing your teeth – it was very memorable, almost like a statement of defiance for Nineties youth. I remember thinking that line *"Sleep around/If we like"* was very defiant, and hoping that the song would be a massive hit, thinking that it should be if there was any justice in the world.'

Was the band disappointed not to be Number One?

'Not really, well . . . they were wondering, when it went in at Number 2, but these things don't really phase them.

'A completely fantastic record kept them off the top, of course,' added Simon sarcastically. 'The Outhere Brothers' "Boom Boom Boom". It made me think of Midge Ure – how Joe Dolce's "Shaddap Your Face" kept him from the top . . . the Joe Dolce Music Theatre, he'll go to his grave being pissed off about that.

'For their *Top Of The Pops* appearance,' he continued, 'Gaz had a pearly king style crazy waistcoat, which we tried to convince the press had once belonged to Gary Glitter. Danny and Mickey swapped their instruments around – Mickey on drums was singularly unimpressive and kept missing his cue, and the camera kept panning away quickly. Danny was wearing a cloth cap.'

'Alright' was Radio 1FM's most played

The band on the set for 'Alright' (top) at Port Merion, first made famous by *The Prisoner* (above) with Patrick McGoohan

record for three weeks in a row.

The song was also played live on *Later With Jools Holland*; got used in the promo trailer for *Ruby's Health Quest* on BBC1; ended the year by appearing on the soundtrack to *Clueless*, the new US feelgood teen movie, starring Alicia Silverstone.; and helped inspire a whole clutch of articles in 'serious' papers like *The Times* about the birth of 'happy pop' – as opposed to 'unhappy pop', I guess… although that phrase does seem like a contradiction in terms.

To say that it made a splash would be a bit of an understatement.

'A BIT OF A LAUGH'

THE band themselves were a little worried that the lyrics to 'Alright' might be misconstrued…

'The stuff about *"We are young/We run green,"* Gaz told *Q*, 'isn't about being 19, but really 13 or 14 and just discovering girls and drinking. It's meant to be light-hearted and a bit of a laugh, not a rebellious call to arms.'

'It certainly wasn't written in a very summery vibe,' Danny added. 'It was written in a cottage where the heating had packed up and we were trying to build fires to keep warm.'

Around this time, Supergrass were involved in a bizarre gardening accident while filming for Central Television, in which Mickey was left with a severely bruised arm and in severe doubt as to Gaz's skills as a lawnmower driver.

But the less said about that, the better.

WHAT IS POP? (DEFINITELY THE FINAL REPRISE)

IT seems that almost everyone agrees that in 'Alright' – cheeky two-note barrelhouse piano, lines like *'We are young/We get by/Can't go mad/Ain't got time'*, n'all – Supergrass have created one of THE songs of 1995, a song to rank alongside Pulp's 'Common People' and Oasis' 'Wonderwall', a song to equal any of the pop songs of past years, a song to remember . . . whatever the hell you *want* to remember by it, really.

Getting laid, getting drunk, getting stoned,

More kitsch capers on 'Alright'

getting to stay up all night without drugs, getting to brush your teeth twice daily, getting your first snog, getting to miss the bus, getting to stick two fingers up to authority, getting to go abroad, getting to stay at home, getting to boil the goose and give the sauce to the gander.

Or even…

Getting to do none of the above.

But ain't that what pop's all about?

Three-in-a-bed time

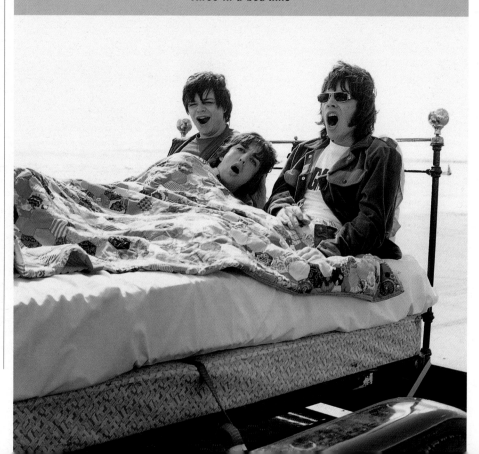

★★★★★☆☆☆☆★★★★★★

Sofa, So Good
Supergrass Take On The World

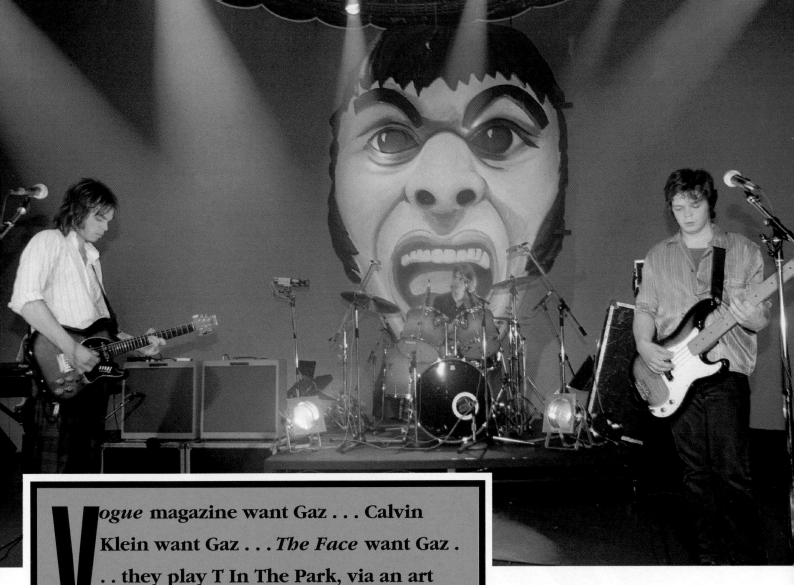

Vogue magazine want Gaz . . . Calvin Klein want Gaz . . . *The Face* want Gaz . . . they play T In The Park, via an art deco factory . . . 'I Should Coco' is shortlisted for the Mercury Music Prize . . . Supergrass tour the US for the third time . . . Mickey talks about the group's future directions . . . and: pop – the final frontier?

'CAUGHT BY THE FUZZ' CAUGHT BY THE FUZZ!

NOT content with reissuing 'Alright' as an 11-track mini-album in Japan, in July Supergrass went back to the States for another 10 dates, and attained instant notoriety by attempting to use the police mugshot of the disgraced Hugh Grant after his arrest on posters promoting the just reissued 'Caught By The Fuzz' US single.

Unfortunately, the posters had to be withdrawn.

'Basically we could have been horribly sued,' a spokesman explained. 'In the States there's a privacy law which means you own your own image and anybody else is not allowed to use it without your consent. Funnily enough, I don't think the band had Hugh's consent! It was just general cheekiness.'

A new video for the single – culled by Nick and Dom from Super-8 footage of their previous US tour – was put together at the super-cheap cost of about £2,000. It turned out to be Mickey's favourite to date.

'It has a shot for every line in the song,' the bassist told *The Maker's* News Desk. 'The first line is "Caught by the fuzz", and it has this picture of three New York cops waking along smiling and waving at the camera. It's really cheeky stuff.'

PANTS AND SOCKS

STRANGE stories began to surface all over the media concerning various members of Supergrass – proof that the band were indeed a national phenomenon.

First off, there was a sighting of Gaz in Italian *Vogue*, quickly followed by the news that Calvin Klein wanted the singer to replace rapper Marky Mark as The Face Of The Nineties in their underwear ads. The man they wanted Gaz to strip for was acclaimed photographer Steven Meisel, responsible for Madonna's *Sex* book.

Gaz turned the job down, much to the disappointment of his fellow band-members.

Gaz in Glasgow, T In The Park

Backstage at the T In The Park fest

'It would have kept us in pants and socks for a year,' explained Mickey to the national press. 'Except for Danny. I'm not sure he wears any.'

It wasn't that he was shy ('Gaz has nothing to hide,' his PR department claimed), more cos his schedule was too hectic. The three-day photo shoot in New York clashed with the band's forthcoming tour of Japan.

'SMOULDERING AND HUMBLE'

BY now, even the establishment was starting to catch up.

In August came the news that 'I Should Coco' had been shortlisted as one of the 10 Albums Of The Year in the Mercury Music Awards (the award was eventually won by Portishead's 'Dummy', an album which was released 15 months previously). To celebrate, Parlophone released 'Sofa (Of My Lethargy)' as a limited edition two-track promo CD, and the band performed a strangely lacklustre version of 'We're Not Supposed To' on the BBC2 programme run to tie in with the awards.

The same month, *The Face* named Gaz as Number 86 in the 100 Most Influential People In Fashion, 'for sterling services to the sideboard', and the singer featured in both fashion bible *i-D* and a *Clothes Show* article, with his 'George Best growths'.

The band also appeared on the front of *The Observer's Life* magazine, where Gaz got described as 'the smouldering and humble prodigy, with the stage presence of a 50-year-old jazz legend', Danny as 'the sort of person who could sit on a plane between a nun and a sailor and have them both laughing', and Mickey as 'the earthing presence at 25; the one with a kid, common sense and a beer belly who the other two rib, but adore.'

'Gaz and Danny live together, with Mickey a few doors down,' *The Observer Magazine* wrote, 'It's like *The Breakfast Club*, but with a better soundtrack.'

'People say we're influenced by the Seventies, but we weren't really around for it,' Danny told its journalist. (Gaz and Danny were four and six respectively in 1980.) 'We're more influenced by Seventies retro than the Seventies.'

The next month, *Q*, bang up to date as ever, shoved them on their cover – the ultimate sign that Supergrass had been accepted by the rock hierarchy.

Danny with girlfriend Pearl from Powder

MAYHEM! MADNESS! FESTIVAL MELTDOWN!

STILL in August, Supergrass created scenes of mayhem at Glasgow's T In The Park festival, where they played King Tut's Wah-Wah tent.

Earlier in the day, they'd been driven through the streets of Glasgow in a silver Rolls Royce to Tunnock's art deco factory, where employees and their children were waiting for them at the gates. One small boy was stripped to his waist, revealing a (hopefully) temporary chest tattoo of 'Tunnock's Tea Cakes' and 'Supergrass', surmounted by an illustration of the tea-time snack. Autographs got signed, caramel logs got munched, Mickey got snapped on a small platform of chocolate marshmallows and Danny got to go barefoot. Gaz,

meanwhile, was nowhere to be seen.

Back at the site, the drummer tried to wheedle his way out of the band's signing session – more concerned with snogging his new girlfriend Pearl, the singer from Powder.

'Oh come on Danny, it'll do your ego the world of good,' cajoled Mickey cannily. Danny shrugged, and acquiesced.

When it came close to showtime, insane queues began to stretch from every available opening of the 500-capacity tent, as roughly four times as many people as could see, squashed in to watch Supergrass play in Britain for the first time since their album hit the Number 1spot.

'As soon as it was time for the band to come on, you realised no one was watching Therapy? over at the main stage and everyone was moving as a mass in one

direction towards the tent,' recalled Simon Blackmore. 'The police were blocking all the entrances. You couldn't hear the band from the stage. The only thing the band themselves could hear were people singing, and they could see them jumping, and… then they played "Alright". It was tearful, amazing. Somebody remarked that they wouldn't fancy Elastica's chances following them.'

Melody Maker's report was typically succinct:

'If you can remember Supergrass,' the reviewer – well alright, me then – wrote, 'You weren't there. Alright?'

(There was another public sighting of Danny and Pearl a few weeks later at the Reading Festival, where they showed off their matching foot tattoos to anyone who was interested, and spent the rest of the time snogging – which led to cruel jokes about Pearl's age in the *Maker*, and catty comments like 'I hope she kisses better than she dances' in *Time Out*.

A curious item appeared in *MM*'s Rumour Mill the week after Reading , wherein an apology was ran for saying that Mickey had snogged a girl so hard, she'd fallen backwards and treated everyone to a Bird's Eye view of her Captain's Table.

For, not only is Mickey happily monogamous and a father to boot, he wasn't even there!)

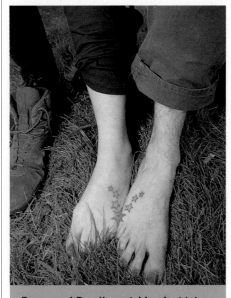

Danny and Pearl's matching foot tatoos

A view from the drumstool, US tour, September 1995

LIPSTICK AND FASHION

TOWARDS the end of 1995, Supergrass toured the States for a third time, playing much bigger venues. The tour started in Atlanta, a Fifties kind of town with dusty old buildings, and proceeded to Cleveland, where Supergrass played a 'cool' gay club, with people in S&M gear. By now, girls were throwing their knickers and bras on stage, with phone numbers written on them in lipstick (a far cry from the days when The Jennifers used to beg girls for their phone numbers after shows!).

The band did the usual round of interviews for the US music press, even doing a seven-page fashion feature for the October issue of prestigious US magazine, *Rolling Stone*.

'We draw on music from different ages,' Mickey told one US publication, 'it's like reading just one book. You should read gobs of books. It's loads more interesting.'

'It's good coming out here because it's like when we were starting out in Britain,' Gaz told the *NME*'s news desk in August. 'Not a lot of people know about us and we enjoy that. We've been having some good times. San Francisco is great, man. It's got a good vibe and the women are beautiful. We've been at these truck stops as well. But when we go there we get these six foot wide redneck American guys staring us up, which is wild man, giving us wolf whistles. And we get these old women saying "You in a rock band?" and asking for autographs.'

After the States, the band played their first Japanese dates – in Tokyo, Nagova and Osaka, from September 25th onwards.

SO – WHAT OF THE FUTURE...

SUPERGRASS' second album has already partially been written, but the band have no idea what it'll sound like.

'It won't be string sections and cellos,' Mickey told *Q* in October, 'but then again I wouldn't want to dismiss that completely. You never know what we'll feel like in five years time.'

'It probably won't be a techno record. There'll be a few comedy songs, some punk, some country and western stuff, a bit of JJ Cale, some bitchin' riffs,' offered Danny.

'We've got six new songs and there's a couple we're actually starting to use live now,' Mickey recently told the *Maker's* News Desk. 'We haven't got names for them yet, but there's one we opened at Glastonbury with. It didn't work there cos the sound was so appalling, but we opened with it again at the Roskilde festival in Denmark and it was great. My brother heard it after not hearing us play for two years because he'd been away, and he came up after the gig and said it was the best song in the set.

'We've never really had a direction,' he added. 'It's all swings and roundabouts with us, it all goes in different ways. The new songs are really, really diverse. There's one that's like Elvis Costello-ish reggae or something, with lots of rock'n'roll licks going on as well.

'There's a weird funk song going down that's really slow and meandering, getting towards Portishead territory. There's also a couple of punk riffs that we've got going that have a kind of "Caught By The Fuzz"/Buzzcocks feel to them, and we've got a couple of quiet, acoustic songs as well. We want to get into pre-production on the next album as soon as possible, basically because a lot of the songs on "I Should Coco" have been around a long time and are pretty old to us.'

★★★★★★★★★★★★★★★★

Discography

Parlophone CDR 6396 'Caught By The Fuzz'/'Strange Ones'/'Caught By The Fuzz' (acoustic) *(CD, 10/94)*

Parlophone R 6402 'Mansize Rooster'/'Sitting Up Straight' *(7", first 10,000 red vinyl, then reverts to black vinyl, 2/95, No. 20)*

Parlophone TCR 6402 'Mansize Rooster'/'Sitting Up Straight' *(cassette, 2/95)*

Parlophone CDR 6402 'Mansize Rooster'/'Sitting Up Straight'/'Odd?' *(CD, 2/95)*

Parlophone RS 6410 'Lenny'/'Wait For The Sun' *(7", blue vinyl, numbered, 5/95, No. 9)*

Parlophone TCR 6410 'Lenny'/'Wait For The Sun' *(cassette, 5/95)*

Parlophone CDR 6410 'Lenny'/'Wait For The Sun'/'Sex!' *(CD, 5/95)*

Parlophone R 6413 'Alright'/'Time' *(7", orange vinyl, gatefold sleeve, 7/95, No. 2)*

Parlophone TCR 6413 'Alright'/'Time' *(cassette, 7/95)*

Parlophone CDR 6413 'Alright'/'Time'/'Condition'/'Je Suis Votre Papa Sucre' *(CD, 7/95)*

THE JENNIFERS SINGLES

Nude NUD 2T 'Just Got Back Today'/'Rocks And Boulders'/'Danny's Song'/'Tomorrow's Rain' *(12", 8/92)*

Nude NUD 2CD 'Just Got Back Today'/'Rocks And Boulders'/'Danny's Song'/'Tomorrow's Rain' *(CD, 8/92)*

THE JENNIFERS ON COMPILATION CD

Amber MACH 1CD 'Days Spent Dreaming' (includes one track, 'Tightrope') *(CD, 10/93)*

SUPERGRASS SINGLES

Backbeat (no cat. no.) 'Caught By The Fuzz'/'Strange Ones' *(7", 1,000 only, no p/s, demo recording, 8/94)*

Backbeat (no cat. no.) 'Mansize Rooster'/'Sitting Up Straight' *(7", green vinyl, 500 only, printed Fifties style green cardboard or plain die-cut sleeve, demo recording, 10/94)*

Parlophone R 6396 'Caught By The Fuzz'/'Strange Ones' *(7", 10/94, No. 43)*

Parlophone TCR 6396 'Caught By The Fuzz'/'Strange Ones' *(cassette, 10/94)*

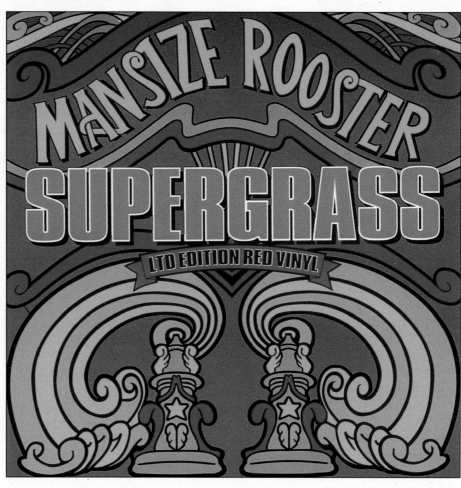

Parlophone 12RDJ 6396 'Caught By The Fuzz'/'Strange Ones'/'Caught By The Fuzz' (acoustic) *(promo 12", title/logo sleeve, 10/94)*

Parlophone 12RDJ 6402 'Mansize Rooster'/'Sitting Up Straight'/'Odd?' *(promo 12", p/s, 2/95)*

Parlophone CDRDJ 6402 'Mansize Rooster'/'Sitting Up Straight'/'Odd?' *(promo CD, p/s, 2/95)*

* GIVIT 10 'Radio 1FM Sessions Vol. 2' *(Vox giveaway cassette, includes one track, 'Sitting Up Straight'(Mark Radcliffe session), 3/95)*

Sub Pop SP 281 'Lose It'/'Caught By The Fuzz '(acoustic) *(USA 7", 2,500 only, on yellow vinyl, 3/95, No. 75. Also included in 'Helter Shelter' Sub Pop Singles Club 4 x 7" box set with booklet, 7/95. A test pressing in stickered plain sleeve was also made, 50 copies)*

Parlophone (no cat. no.) 'I Should Coco' *(a promotional cassette with different inlay, 4/95)*

SUPERGRASS ALBUM

Track listing: 'I'd Like To Know'/'Caught By The Fuzz'/'Mansize Rooster'/'Alright'/'Lose It'/'Lenny'/'Strange Ones'/'Sitting Up Straight'/'She's So Loose'/'We're Not Supposed To'/'Time'/'Sofa (Of My Lethargy)'/'Time To Go'

Parlophone PCSX 7373 'I Should Coco' *(LP, 5,000 only with free 7", 'Stone Free' (live)/'Odd?'(John Peel session), 5/95, No. 1)*

Parlophone TCPCS 7373 'I Should Coco' *(cassette, 5/95)*

Parlophone CDPCS 7373 'I Should Coco' *(CD, 5/95)*

MISCELLANEOUS
(PROMOS/IMPORTS/RARITIES etc)

* (no cat. no.) 'Caught By The Fuzz'/'Mansize Rooster'/'Alright'/'Sitting Up Straight'/'Lose It'/'Strange Ones' *(cassette, original 6 track demo tape, 25 copies, printed sleeve, 7/94)*

Fierce Panda NING 2 'Crazed & Confused' *(double 7" EP, 1,000 only, includes 'Caught By The Fuzz'(demo), 9/94)*

The band backstage at the Boardwalk, Manchester

Parlophone GRASS 1 'I Should Coco' 4 track sampler *(promo CD, black lojo digipak sleeve, 4/95. Also issued in Europe in orange logo digipak sleeve)*

Parlophone 12RDJ 6410 'Lenny'/'Wait For The Sun'/'Sex!' *(promo 12", p/s, 5/95)*

Parlophone CDRDJ 6410 'Lenny'/'Wait For The Sun'/'Sex! ' *(promo CD, p/s, 5/95)*

Fierce Panda NONGCD 1 'Nings Of Desire' *(CD, includes one track, 'Odd?' 5/95)*

* (no cat. no.) 'Melody Maker Six Pack' *(Melody Maker giveaway cassette, includes one track, 'Sitting Up Straight' (Mark Radcliffe session), 6/95)*

Parlophone 12RDJ 6413 'Alright'/'Time'/'Condition'/'Je Suis Votre Papa Sucre' *(promo 12", p/s, 7/95)*

Parlophone CDRDJ 6413 'Alright'/'Time' *(promo CD, black logo digipak sleeve, 7/95.*

Also issued in Europe in green logo digipak sleeve)

EMI Toshiba TOCP-8631 'Alright'/'Condition'/'Je Suis Votre Papa Sucre'/'Lenny' (single edit)/'Wait For The Sun'/'Sex!'/'Odd?' (live)/'She's So Loose' (live)/'Strange Ones' (live)/'Where Have All The Good Times Gone?' (live)/'Lose It' (live) *(Japanese 11 track CD, lyric insert, p/s, 7/95)*

Music Prize Ltd MMP CD4 '1995 Mercury Music Prize - Ten Albums Of The Year ' *(CD, includes one track, 'Sofa (Of My Lethargy)' (radio edit), 8/95)*

Parlophone GRASS 2 'Sofa (Of My Lethargy)' (radio edit)/'Sofa (Of My Lethargy)' (album version) *(promo CD, p/s, 8/95)*

Ablex MM/BBCCD 97/99 'Hold On - BBC

Radio 1FM Sessions' *(CD, includes one track, 'Odd?' (John Peel session), 9/95)*

Capitol CDEST 2267 'Clueless' (Original Soundtrack) *(CD, includes one track, 'Alright', 10/95)*

Capitol CDESTDJ 2267 'Clueless' (Original Soundtrack) *(6 track promo CD, p/s, includes one track, 'Alright', 10/95)*

FANZINES

Mansize c/o Sophie Everest, 37 Christchurch Road, Oxton, Birkenhead L43 5SS, £1 (0151 670 1418)

Coconuts c/o A Nunn, 3 Dalnavert, King Craig, Invernesshire, PH21 1NQ, £1.50 (01540 651403)

You can write to Supergrass for information at PO Box 2212, Reading RG1 4YH